86-10-09

D1252211

RENAISSANCE PARIS

DAVID THOMSON

View of the Tuileries

RENAISSANCE PARIS

Architecture and Growth 1475–1600

David Thomson

UNIVERSITY OF CALIFORNIA PRESS

BERKELEY AND LOS ANGELES

for Catherine

COPYRIGHT © 1984 A. ZWEMMER LTD

UNIVERSITY OF CALIFORNIA PRESS

BERKELEY AND LOS ANGELES, CALIFORNIA

PRINTED IN GREAT BRITAIN AT THE CAMELOT PRESS LTD, SOUTHAMPTON

LIBRARY OF CONGRESS CATALOGING IN PUBLICATION DATA

THOMSON, DAVID, 1912–
RENAISSANCE PARIS.

BIBLIOGRAPHY: P.
INCLUDES INDEX.
I. ARCHITECTURE, RENAISSANCE – FRANCE – PARIS.
2. ARCHITECTURE – FRANCE – PARIS.   3. PARIS (FRANCE) – BUILDINGS.
I. TITLE.
NA1050.T53   1984   720'.944'361   84-40286
ISBN 0-520-05347-8
ISBN 0-520-05359-1 (PBK.)

Contents

List of Illustrations

4

5

Acknowledgements

Generous grants from the Leverhulme Foundation and from the British Academy provided the means to work in Paris and to buy research materials in Paris during the 1970s.

For ten years I was guided by the late Professor Anthony Blunt, who cleared obstacles in the way of progress on this and other projects. The importance of his inspiration has been incalculable, and his friendship and wisdom will be missed by many students of French and Italian art and architecture. This book would not have been written so soon, nor in its present form, without the cooperation and enthusiasm for the subject of A. Don Johnson. His reconstruction drawings in Chapter IV have made it possible to analyse the styles of later sixteenth-century Parisian hôtels free from long explanatory footnotes on sources, and in many fewer words of text than would have been needed without his meticulous work. I am deeply grateful to him for his dedicated effort, which has brought an important part of the architectural history of Paris to life.

In Paris I owe a great deal to the advice, help and kindness of Monsieur Jean Pierre Babelon, Madame Françoise Boudon, Madame Catherine Grodecki, Madame Dominique Hervier and Monsieur Claude Mignot. The unrestricted hospitality of Jeffrey Kime has made all my visits to Paris memorable and exciting. In England the counsels of Rosalys Coope, Mary Whiteley, John Onians and John Mitchell have been invaluable. I have been fortunate to have Desmond Zwemmer and John Taylor as my publishers for their understanding and skill in turning a disorderly typescript into an attractive book. Stella Shackle and Michael Brandon-Jones have taken and made up most of the photographs, often at short notice, and their professionalism has been of considerable help. I am grateful to Juliet Fulford for assistance with last minute problems.

Introduction

If Louis XI's inclination to make Tours the permanent capital of France in the 1470s had become a reality, the architectural history of Paris would be very different.[1] The gravitation of the Court, its personalities and developing institutions towards Paris, accounts for the building of the great majority of the noble town houses described in these pages. Few of the great or the wealthy who built houses in Paris during the sixteenth century were Parisian by origin or by adoption, and makes the declaration by François I of 1528 that Paris was to become his 'résidence habituelle' or base especially significant.[2] The consequences of the King's decision were not immediate, for he did not follow his announcement with any building initiative, but the peripatetic life of the Court had shifted finally from the pleasures of the Loire Valley to the Ile de France where during the second half of his reign François I built at Fontainebleau, Saint Germain en Laye, Villers Cotterets and just west of Paris in the Bois de Boulogne.[3] The final confirmation of the King's intention to root his dynasty in Paris came in the 1540s with his rationalization of Royal properties within the walls by selling off for development the large and unwanted Hôtel de Flandre in the north and the Hôtel Saint-Pol in the east of the city.[4] These and other important *lotissements* of land belonging to churches within the medieval walls would not have been commercially successful, and have led to rapid and widespread bourgeois and aristocratic building in the late 1540s up to the late 1580s without the King's public and private initiatives. It might be argued that the history of French institutions and of the Church diminishes the significance of the King's action; the Exchequer (Chambre des Comptes) was installed on the Ile de la Cité, the Parlement de Paris had for long been the senior legal and judicial body of the Kingdom and it was only in Paris that each bishop and archbishop kept or had had built a residence.[5] Paris was the capital in practice, but the final confirmation of the city's primacy in the realm was the building of the new Louvre, the nexus of monarch and capital. This marriage of the last Valois Kings with Paris was not as immediate nor as decisive as François I's proclamation might lead us to suppose. French Kings to the end of the Ancien Régime could be circumspect if not hostile towards their capital, but not always as consistently suspicious as Louis XIV. Between his announcement of 1528 and the 1540s François I did nothing more than pull down the keep which filled the greater part of the courtyard of the old Louvre. He said he felt 'at home' at Fontainebleau,[6] where there was security, comfort and good hunting, and as a result of this preference the Chancellery, Cardinals and some nobles opted to build at Fontainebleau around the château during the 1530s and the early 1540s.[7] The form and style of these houses at Fontainebleau have to be considered as a part of the social and architectural history of Paris, as it was the single most significant and active foyer of aristocratic town-house design and building before the shift, apart from helping to fill one of a number of serious gaps in our knowledge of developments in Paris.

An introduction is not the place to discourage the reader with laments over the large number of important and prestigious lost *hôtels*, whose appearance cannot be reconstructed and whose loss defeats any attempt at a representative chronological or stylistic study of domestic architecture in Renaissance Paris. It is more practicable to plot the history of the growth of the city from plans, surveys and the documents of the notarial archives. The reasons for this survey are straightforward. In the modern literature of Renaissance art or architecture Paris is the Cinderella of the European capitals, in which only the Louvre and sometimes the rebuilt Hôtel Carnavalet and the Hôtel d'Angoulême make an appearance to represent a hundred years of the city's contribution to architectural style. The process of discovering more of the buildings, their decoration, function and equipment goes on, and more substantial contributions will be produced by French scholars in the years to come, but the fruits of modern research when published are dispersed and little noticed by the non-specialist. Much of the following text is a work of synthesis, which is an attempt to make known a fascinating chapter in architectural history to the English-speaking reader and is a tribute to the work of my friends in Paris.

London 1982

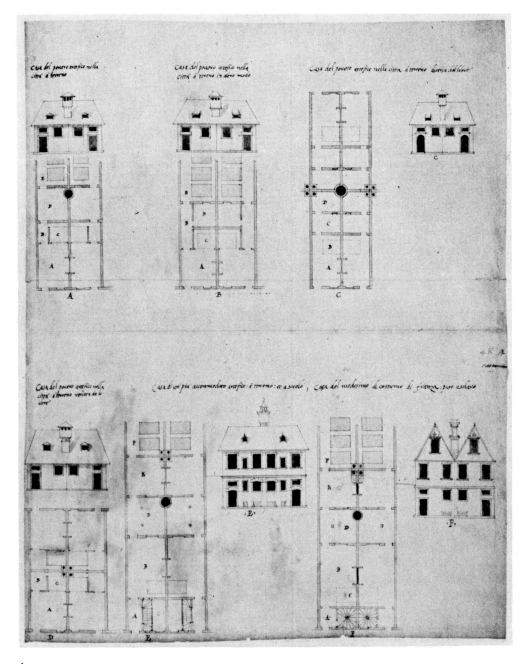

1
Sebastiano Serlio: Houses for artisans in the Italian and French manner. (Avery ms. n° XLVIII)

CHAPTER I

Style and Topography

1 Corrozet, Serlio, Androuet du Cerceau and de l'Orme

In 1550 Gilles Corrozet in his *Antiquitez et Singularitez de Paris, ville capitale du Royaume de France* wrote: 'There are a large number of houses [in Paris] which have declined as the times have changed and are now in the hands of others: for once there was not a Prince, Lord nor Prelat in France including the twelve Peers of the Realm who did not have a town house, because it was here as a rule that the King held Court. There are in our day some remarkable buildings in the Romanesque, Greek and Modern styles and I shall let you have the names of these for there are too many important houses to count: and every day the building of new houses goes on, which makes me believe that the City of Paris will never be completed.'[1] Around 1608 Malherbe in a letter to Peiresc wrote: 'If you come back to Paris in two years' time you will not recognize it.' Natives and foreigners wrote much in praise of the city during the sixteenth century but never go into any detail on the style and function of the buildings which in their eyes were contributing so much to the prestige and embellishment of the city. The earliest and most intriguing description of the style and function of an ideal gentleman's house came from Corrozet in 1539; a house which faced east to enjoy the sunrise, built of at least two types of good quality dressed stone including marble, with an imposing door either as an entrance gateway or on the body of the house itself, and numerous other features of note such as a forecourt paved in marble and a garden court.[2] The physiognomy of the house described by Corrozet might be imagined in a number of ways by the reader, but his house may well correspond to an early 'classic' Parisian town house on a rectangular site with the main block set between forecourt and garden and hidden from the street by an entrance screen. Corrozet does not describe the architecture of the elevations of his 'Invention Joyeuse', whether it is Gothic or Classical, Romanesque, Greek or Modern, but in one line he describes it as a 'Maison de pris, bien paincte à l'antiquaille', and later when he talks of the beauties of the garden front he lists medallions and statues both ancient and modern. The irony of Corrozet's long description is that it contains little or nothing for the architectural historian interested in plans and elevations, but it is a rare view in detail of a prestigious house through the eyes of a sixteenth-century Parisian. Apart from the quality of the materials and noting the developed artistic tastes of the owner, Corrozet was more at pains to describe the fittings of each room from the master bedroom to the kitchen. The first published guide to the City of Paris and its monuments was Corrozet's *Fleur des Antiquitez . . . de Paris* of 1539 which gives the reader an agreeable historical and topographical account of the various 'quartiers' and some of their buildings, in which Corrozet shows no more interest or awareness of the changes from the Gothic to the 'classic' and classical in the town houses of his times. Contemporary printed texts are of limited value in the history of the Parisian *hôtel*, and so another class of book needs to be exploited, the architectural pattern books of Sebastiano Serlio (1475–1553) and of Jacques Androuet du Cerceau (c. 1510–1585) and the architectural treatises of Philibert de l'Orme (1505/1510–1570).

Serlio's life, career and 'literary remains' have been amply described elsewhere and there is more to come,[3] but for our purposes it is the last decade of his life spent in France preparing his pattern book *On Domestic Architecture* which is our first graphic and systematic evidence of the forms and styles of town houses interpreted by an Italian 'in modo di Francia' (Figs 1–5). Serlio's drawings of the plans and elevations of town houses in the Italian and French idioms are rightly said to be ideal rather than actual schemes, but his houses in the French idiom are based on unidentified and lost houses which he had studied at Paris and Fontainebleau from 1541 to 1546. The perfect regularity of the sites seen in Serlio's plans precludes any possibility that they are records of houses seen by Serlio, for regular sites were almost unknown in the built up areas within the city walls, and his drawings predate the development of the large *lotissements* of the later 1540s and 1550s which will be described below. The town houses drawn by Serlio range from houses for the poor artisan on to or up to houses for rich merchants, but Serlio cannot have been focusing on Paris when he wrote that the dwellings of the poorest men are located in the suburbs close to the city near the gates and therefore near to the markets and fairs. In the Paris of the early sixteenth century, with the exception of the streets nearest to the Louvre, the affluent and rich were distinguished only by the number of plots and of houses which they had acquired in comparison to their poorer neighbours. Serlio's syntheses of the artisans' and the merchants' houses summarize and rationalize some planning and building traditions known to have existed in Paris before he came to France, but the greater part of his book *On Domestic Architecture* deals with town and country houses for noble gentlemen, Princes and Kings. It is in these drawings of noble and princely houses that we find ideas and ideals of plan and of elevation which set revised standards for Parisian master masons and architects and created new ambitions and fashions amongst patrons. The remarkable feature of this class of designs by Serlio is how well they anticipated the new architectural opportunities of the *lotissements* of the mid and late 1540s.

Serlio never categorized or fully described his thoughts on the problems of building in towns, especially French towns, but scattered through his

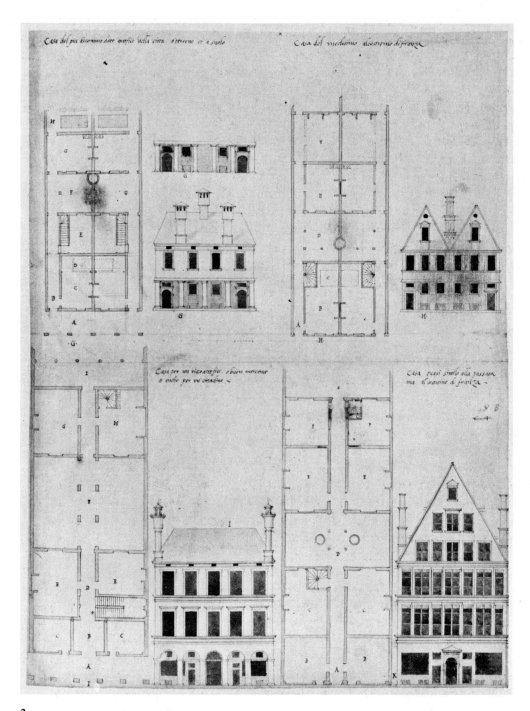

2
Sebastiano Serlio: Houses for boûrgeois in the Italian and French manner. (Avery ms. n° XLIX)

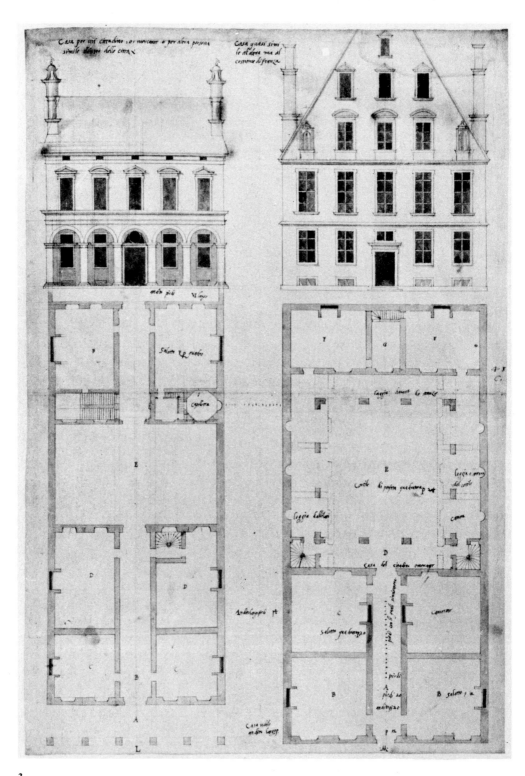

3
Sebastiano Serlio: Houses for wealthy bourgeois in the Italian and French manner. (Avery ms. n° L)

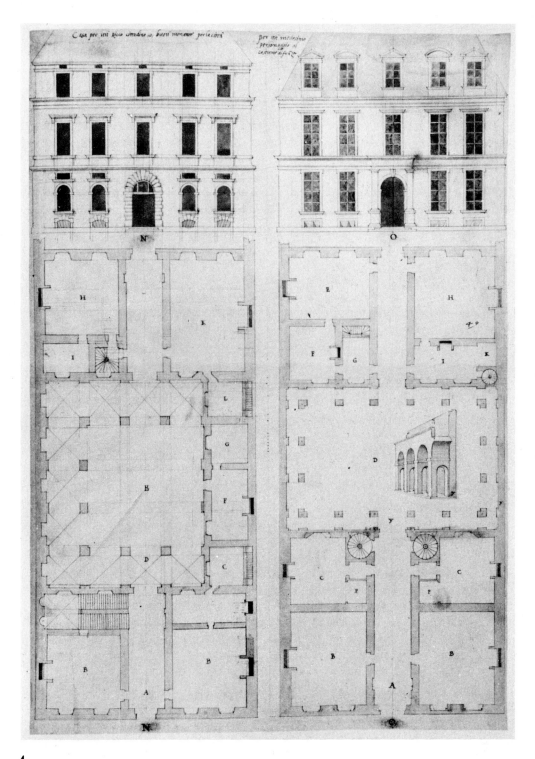

4
Sebastiano Serlio: Houses for rich bourgeois in the Italian and French manner. (Avery ms. n° LI)

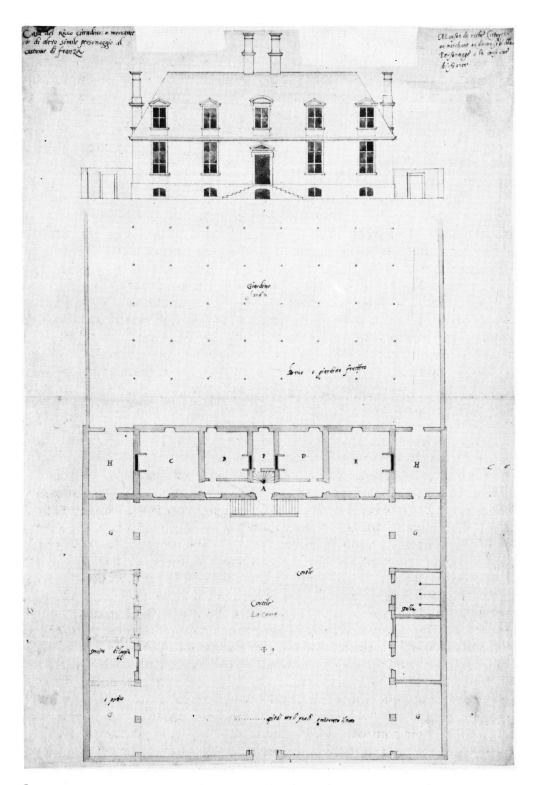

5
Sebastiano Serlio: House for a rich citizen or merchant in the French manner. (Avery ms. n° IV)

writings is a series of remarks which when collected give a fascinating insight into the relationship of patron, architect and builder, and of building tradition and styles at Fontainebleau and Paris. He insisted that the architect's first duty was to please his patron, and '. . . la casa e fatta prima per la commoditta: piu per che pei Decoro . . .' Serlio had a keen sense of stylistic decorum which decisively influenced French writers on architecture up to the eighteenth century and which can be seen in some Parisian *hôtels* begun before his death. His thoughts on the decoration of the elevations of a building were both hierarchical and empirical; the most elaborate ornament (and by implication the most pretentious) on town houses should be reserved for the very great of the land, with the houses of those of lesser social rank, however wealthy, bearing fewer if any classical and armorial adornments. The empirical side of Serlio's thought is found in his acceptance and appreciation of window spacings which catered to the needs of the rooms inside, before a 'concordant disharmony'[4], before any requirement for regularity or exact symmetry of both halves of an elevation, and which he noted as a likeable quality in French building, '. . . where people like licentious things more than regular things.' Tall dormers were a happy French invention in Serlio's eyes, in the way in which they crowned a building, and as we know from other kinds of writing from the period, a building's imposing silhouette contributed to its romantic appeal. The decorative systems on the buildings in Serlio's drawings were no more than proposals in his mind, and were not intended as samples of model applied architecture in a dogmatic neo-classical sense. The design and proportions of decorative details and the size and use of rooms were decisions which would finally lie with the patron whom, he knew from his own experience, was likely to have opinions on such matters.

The number of drawings in the two manuscripts of Serlio's book which can be reliably associated with private houses at Fontainebleau and Paris is small. In the text which accompanies the sixth drawing in the Avery Library manuscript, Serlio summarizes the character of the houses built in and around Fontainebleau during the reign of François I as '. . . case continuare in longezza . . .' (Fig. 5). Here the site is broad and rectangular with the main block or *corps de logis* built across the middle. The elevation is simple but not austere with a tall 'piano nobile' over the basement offices and stores. The pitch of the roof starts from a cornice, and the dormers are given alternating triangular and curved pediments. A double ramp central staircase leads into the vestibule from the courtyard and garden sides, and access to the attic floor is by the two spiral staircases in the small angle pavilions in the left- and right-hand corners of the courtyard. In a much quoted phrase, Serlio wrote that an outstanding quality he found in French houses was their comfort, which might be interpreted as their practicality, and we can follow in this plan the arrangements for the service functions, and the partition of the public from the private life of a Bellifontaine or Parisian house to which Serlio alludes. Corrozet spoke of the pleasure of the sunrise, and this typical *hôtel* from Serlio shows a well-lit *corps de logis* only one room deep, an enfilade which had become standard by his day and was to remain in favour up to the late seventeenth century. Compared with Paris during the first three decades of the sixteenth century, building at Fontainebleau during the 1540s took place in more favourable conditions on large green field sites around the château and we shall see how these standards created higher expectations for building in the capital.

The most prolific popularizer of architectural design of Renaissance France, Jacques Androuet du Cerceau the Elder, owned or borrowed the Avery Library manuscript of Serlio's book. Du Cerceau plagiarized a great deal from Serlio, and his first *Livre d'Architecture* published in Paris in 1559 owes its format but few of its fifty designs to the Italian. The schemes in du Cerceau's book are all in a distinctively French manner but the book is most remarkable for the variety and fancy of its plans of the large scale buildings with square, rectangular, circular, cruciform and octagonal courtyards. The large ideal schemes may well have impressed Parisian builders and patrons with the systems of the elevations, but it is amongst the smaller projects at the beginning of du Cerceau's suite that we should look for plans which might have been conceived with Paris in mind, or more probably were based on recent Parisian buildings. The first and smallest of du Cerceau's series (Figs 8–9) for a person of 'moyen estat' is a design for a *corps de logis*, without any subordinate buildings or topographical context, but this is the sort of structure to be expected on a rectangular city site, on a thoroughfare.

The plans of the basement, ground and first floors of this house provide an interesting social insight, with unlit cellars below ground, a ground floor where the whole of the left half is taken up with the kitchen which is evidence of a traditional bourgeois social priority, and the first flight of the main staircase leading to a first floor with from left to right a *chambre* (Cubiculum), *garderobe* (Vestiarium), or wardrobe and a *salle* (Aula) or hall, which would have been the living room cum dining room. The *chambre* with its wardrobe would have been the owner's apartment with the hall across the landing as the only reception room of the house. The use of the attic floor is not specified by du Cerceau, but it would be used conventionally for children or servants. This scheme is a perfect example of French 'comfort' as understood and interpreted by Serlio. The windows are arranged so as to give each room light in its middle, rather than any effort being made at strict uniform balance in the elevations. The street front has raised lights to keep out the gaze of the curious passerby from the kitchen and the other room on the right of the ground floor, which would have been a convenient place of business for the bourgeois. The small raised cabinets on the back of the house were to become a popular feature for courtyard and garden fronts well into the reign of Louis XIV, and inside they were rarely much larger than the five feet square in du Cerceau's design. Such tiny rooms were to be found in both town and

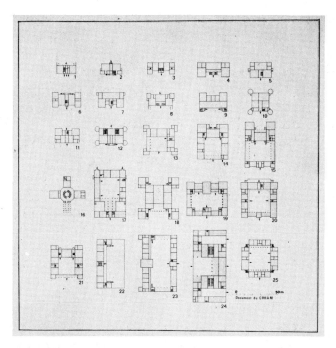

6
Scale plans of projects 1 to
25 of Androuet du
Cerceau's *Livre
d'Architecture* of 1559.
Drawing by Monsieur Jean
Blécon of CRHAM, Paris.

7
Scale plans of projects 26 to
50 of Androuet du
Cerceau's *Livre
d'Architecture* of 1559.
Drawing by Monsieur Jean
Blécon of CRHAM, Paris.

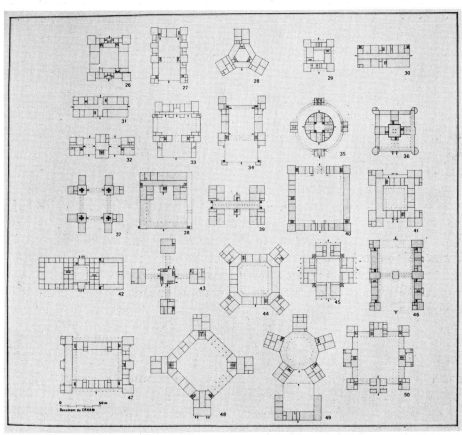

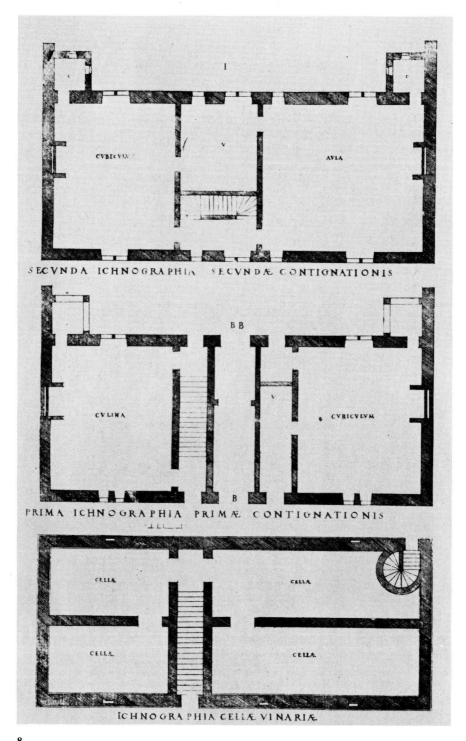

SECVNDA ICHNOGRAPHIA SECVNDÆ CONTIGNATIONIS

PRIMA ICHNOGRAPHIA PRIMÆ CONTIGNATIONIS

ICHNOGRAPHIA CELLÆ VINARIÆ

8

Androuet du Cerceau: Plan of Project I from the *Livre d'Architecture* of 1559. Cellars at the bottom, ground floor in the middle and first-floor plan at the top of the engraving.

FACIES ANTERIOR IN VIAM SPECTANS

LITERA NOTATA B

FACIES POSTERIOR IN AREAM SPECTANS

NOTATA LITERA B

9
Androuet du Cerceau: Street and courtyard elevations of Project I from the *Livre d'Architecture* of 1559.

country houses as the inner sanctum of the owner for work, study, prayer or as a strong room for his valuables.

Du Cerceau's designs XIII, XIIII and XXI show the most common form of house in the *Livre d'Architecture* (Figs 10–13) where he explores the possibilities and varieties of square and rectangular sites. Whether he thought of them as town or country houses is irrelevant, for with minor alterations such as the removal of the angle pavilions on XIII, their size and concentration of living and service parts made them suitable propositions for either a château or an *hôtel*. The *corps de logis* of XIII is of five regular bays and two floors of equal height on the courtyard, with one bay blocked out at the back. This adjustment was made at the back because of the different widths of the lateral wings of the courtyard. The *corps de logis* is an enfilade one room deep entered on both floors from a ramp staircase in the right-hand corner of the court, which divides the hall and apartments from the kitchen, servants' rooms and the latrines. The truly prestigious features of this house are the battlemented entrance screen with its rusticated arch and statues, and on the left of the courtyard the arcaded gallery at the end of which was the seclusion of a small chapel or oratory. The arcade of the gallery would have been used for stores, horses and carriages, and as shelter from the rain for the attendants of a visiting dignitary. This house has a clearly organized circulation. The division between the owners and the servants is more pronounced in XIIII (Fig. 11) where two small open spaces or areas separate the *corps de logis* from the kitchen wing on the left and from the stable wing on the right. The windows in the *corps de logis* facing these small interior courts shows that they were open spaces, but the windows faced a screen to protect the ladies from a view of the kitchen staff and from the sight of the stable's lavatories. The divorce of the main block from the service buildings allows a perfectly symmetrical arrangement of rooms with access from left and right of the courtyard, rather than the one route offered in XIII. XIIII is a scheme for a substantial house, and was most suited to the city with its incorporation of the stables, which at a country house would be farther removed. We know from seventeenth-century opinion of the dislike of cooking smells amongst the nobility,[5] and from these plans the dislike was as pronounced in the sixteenth century with kitchens removed as far as possible from the main house.

The classical trappings of the elevations of houses of this scale in du Cerceau's book are limited to arcading for galleries, friezes and cornices to divide the floors, and pedimented dormers. Only on houses of a very grand aristocratic or Royal scale such as XXII (Fig. 14) do systems of columns or pilasters appear on a *corps de logis*. The preceding scheme (Fig. 13) which has much in common with XIII and XIIII has an austere architecture on the lateral wings and main block, to contrast with an entrance screen (Fig. 12) which is like a *cryptoporticus* without the requisite floor above. Its depth would have made it a public utility on a rainy day, instead of the more familiar form of entrance screen wall with its military

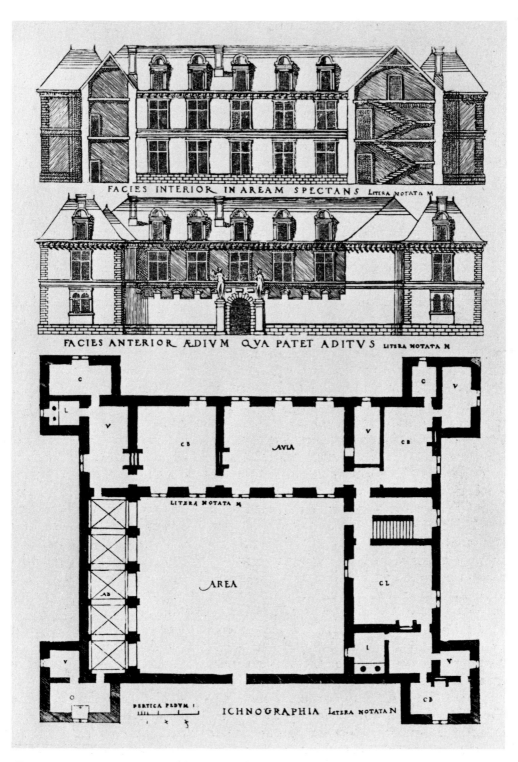

FACIES INTERIOR IN AREAM SPECTANS LITERA NOTATA M

FACIES ANTERIOR ÆDIVM QVA PATET ADITVS LITERA NOTATA N

ICHNOGRAPHIA LITERA NOTATA N

10
Androuet du Cerceau: Project XIII from the *Livre d'Architecture* of 1559.

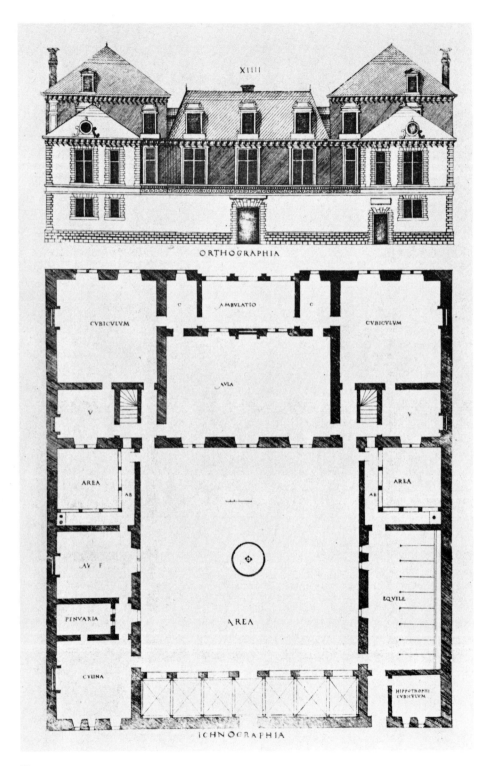

11
Androuet du Cerceau: Project XIIII from the *Livre d'Architecture* of 1559.

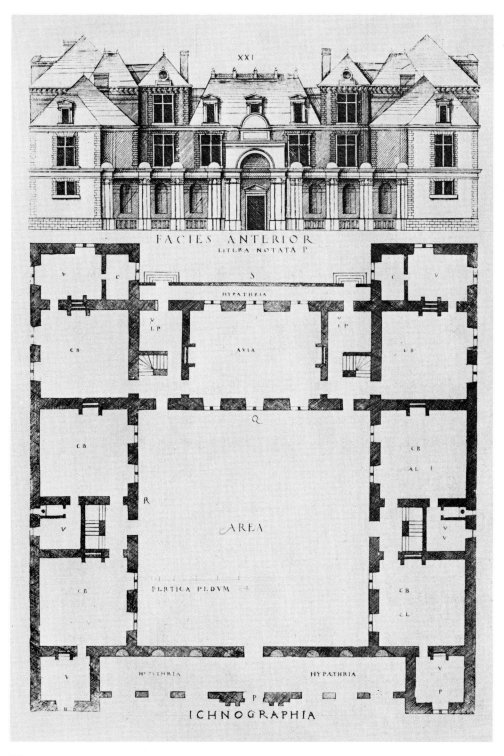

12
Androuet du Cerceau: Project XXI from the *Livre d'Architecture* of 1559.

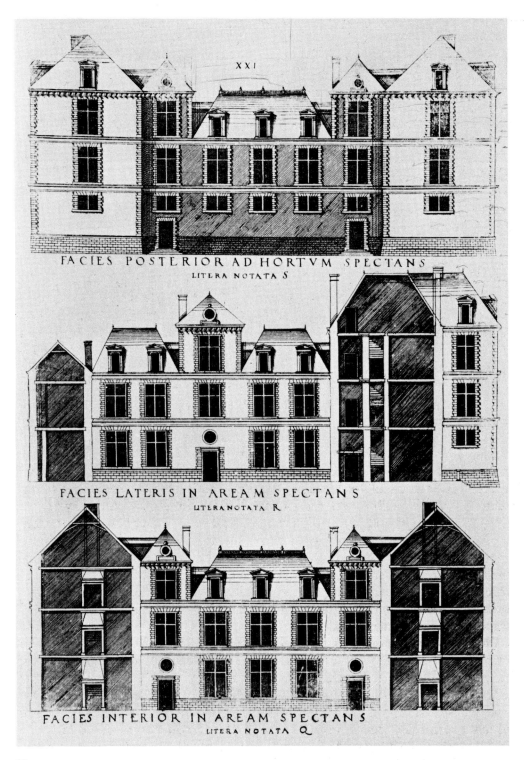

FACIES POSTERIOR AD HORTVM SPECTANS
LITERA NOTATA S

FACIES LATERIS IN AREAM SPECTANS
LITERANOTATA R

FACIES INTERIOR IN AREAM SPECTANS
LITERA NOTATA Q

13
Androuet du Cerceau: Back elevation, lateral and middle sections of Project XXI from the *Livre d'Architecture of 1559*.

crenellation or rustication. As portrayed by du Cerceau, the square courtyarded house is shown as a flexible form of plan, suitable for a strictly hierarchical society, and in which the components could be treated in various contrasting manners.

If Androuet du Cerceau's plates in the 1559 *Livre d'Architecture* give us a fine repertoire of house planning and style from the 1550s, shorn of the Roman and Venetian style villas, castles and palaces which complete Serlio's offering of domestic design, the Frenchman provides not one word of stylistic theory or advice. His foreword to the notices describing each building is concerned only with describing the *toise* (1·959 metres), the statutory unit of measurement, and costing for building contracts in Paris with regional variations. The notices on each building of the *Livre d'Architecture* are dry and to the point, with the total number of *toises* required given at the end for the reader to calculate the cost at the current prices, the first and cheapest has a total of 539 *toises*, 16 *pieds*, XXIII and XXIIII have 2610 and 2750 *toises* respectively, and the fiftieth and largest scheme at the end of the book has 9110 *toises*. Reading du Cerceau's text and browsing through the plates the modern reader can see du Cerceau keeping elaborate detail to a minimum even in the larger projects. His sense of the practical led him to publish a *Second Livre d'Architecture* two years later in 1561, where he illustrates elaborate and costly designs for fireplaces, doorways and dormer windows, presumably for those who have avoided trouble with their masonry contract, and might wish to add some ornate detail.

By an edict of 1557, Henri II sought to standardize Parisian methods of costing a building.[6] The Parisian convention had been to price a wall on its length, height and depth, with any decorative elements such as an architrave counted as double the unit price, and without a reduction being made for voids such as doors and windows. The Royal edict required a new system in which the voids were accounted for and deducted, and applied decorative elements such as simple pilasters, friezes and cornices were included and specified in the price for the wall. The consequence of the new regulation was that a master mason was reluctant to agree to, or to observe the finer decorative points which might be given in an architect's drawing, and a separate agreement on the basis of an agreed and initialled drawing was recommended.

Philibert de l'Orme was the only author on architecture to speak with both theoretical and technical authority in his *Premier Tome d'Architecture* of 1567 and his *Nouvelles Inventions pour bien bastir* of 1561. In Paris he was the architect of the Tuileries palace for Catherine de Medici and of a small number of lost and unrecorded 'hôtels'.[7] In his books he had little to say which specifically concerns the topographical conditions of building in Paris, on the styles, types and configurations of town house building of his times. His thoughts on style and his expertise in building techniques and engineering are woven into an account of the châteaux designed by himself

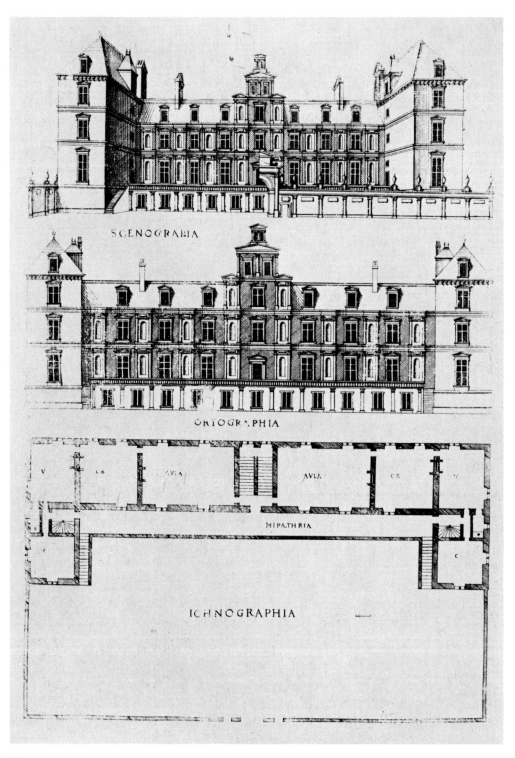

14
Androuet du Cerceau: Project XXII from the *Livre d'Architecture* of 1559.

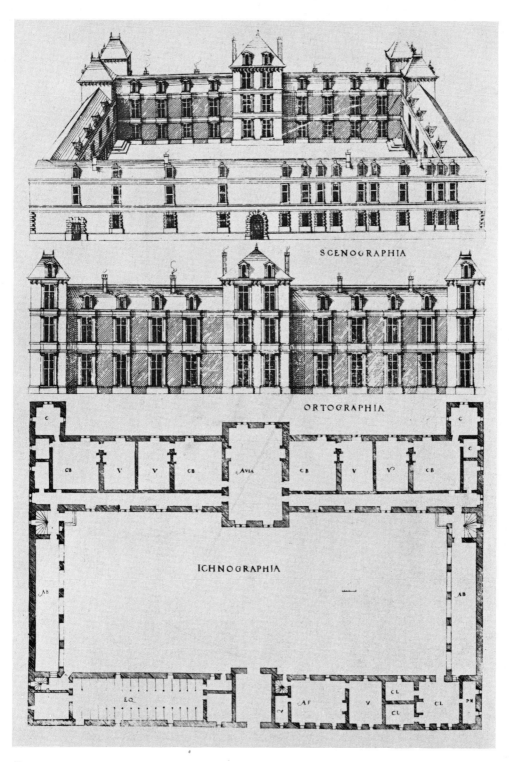

15
Androuet du Cerceau: Project XXIII from the *Livre d'Architecture* of 1559.

29

during the late 1540s and 1550s, and much of his description of building techniques is useful in an account and description of Parisian houses of the last quarter of the sixteenth century, in particular the complicated masonry of suspended cabinets and his carpentry ideas for economical pitched roofs. This egocentric and violent man only illustrated and described the house he had built for himself in the rue de la Cerisaie as a contribution to the upper middle-class town house which could be built without unnecessary expense (Figs 92–94). For this we can be grateful because here he addressed himself to the limitations and an appropriate architectural style for a house on a typical plot on one of the Royal *lotissements* at the Hôtel Saint-Pol near the Bastille. The plan of his house on a long-rectangular site is known, and with the three woodcuts of its elevations and with his text, de l'Orme has left both an architect's and an owner's prescription for a good town house of the 1550s, built well and without excessive cost. De l'Orme in the decade when he was building his Parisian *hôtel* accumulated honours from the Court and a sizeable but not excessive fortune. Despite his rise and prestige de l'Orme built a house which was about 13 metres in width, compared to the first and smallest town house in du Cerceau's *Livre d'Architecture* which spanned a site about 22 metres in width. The pattern books of Serlio and of Androuet du Cerceau provide abundant information on form and style which accompanies and complements the development of the Parisian town house, but du Cerceau made no attempt to record the *hôtels* of his native city, which is irritating in a man whose major life's work was a Royal commission to draw and engrave the great country houses of France, *Les plus excellents Bastiments de France*, two volumes of which were published in 1576 and 1579. De l'Orme's books have a wealth of advice on materials and building procedures which helps with an account of sites and building contracts.

2   The *lotissements* and building contracts

Two practical factors conditioned the evolution of the form and style of the sixteenth-century Parisian *hôtel*. The organization of the *lotissements* for building development of the 1540s determined the size and shape of new houses, and the terms and system of costing of the notarial Parisian building contract provide a basis for understanding the stylistic choices available and the decisions made by patrons and architects.

The costs of a new war against the Emperor Charles V is the principal reason given by François I in the edict of the 23 September 1543, for the division into lots and sale of the royal Hôtels de Bourgogne, d'Artois, de Flandre, d'Etampes and Saint-Pol, leaving only the Louvre in the west, and the rambling Hôtel des Tournelles in the east on the north side of the rue Saint Antoine.[8] The expenses of a campaign was the traditional motive for a monarch to sell land, titles and offices, but in this case an unusual

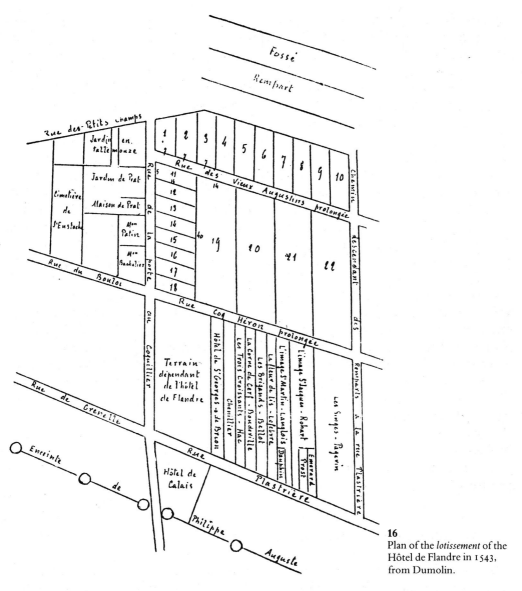

Rue des Petits champs

Fossé

Rempart

Jardin en tallemouze

Jardin de Prat.

Rue des Vieux Augustins prolongée

Cimetière de St Eustache

Maison de Prat

M^{on} Patin

M^{on} Bachelier

Rue de la porte

Rue du Boulot

Rue au Coquillier

Rue Coq Héron prolongée

Terrain dépendant de l'hôtel de Flandre

Rue de Grenelle

Enceinte de

Hôtel de Calais

Rue Plastrière

Philippe Auguste

Descendant des Remparts à la rue Plastrière

Les Singes - Pagevin

Hôtel de St Georges - à J. Bréou

Chanillier

Les Trois Croissants - Hac

La Corne de Cerf - Bondeville

Les Brigands - Bellot

La fleur de lis - Loffevre

L'image St Martin - Lamplois

L'image St Jacques - Rohart

Dauphin

Emerard - Trost

16
Plan of the *lotissement* of the Hôtel de Flandre in 1543, from Dumolin.

rider was included in the text of the edict, that these royal properties were '. . . vieils, inutiles, inhabités et délaissées en ruyne ou décadance . . .' and do nothing more than '. . . encombrer, empescher et defformer grandement la ville de Paris . . .', and these holdings as a result of the royal edict could become '. . . fort propres, utiles, et avesnables a bastir et ediffier plusieurs beaux logis, maisons et demeures'. Not since the Hundred Years War had there been an initiative on the scale and importance of the *lotissement* of the Hôtel Saint-Pol, with its novel straight streets, and at 10 metres in width they were wide for Paris of the period. Medieval royal palaces in Paris, with the exception of the compact Louvre, covered large areas with numerous *corps de logis*, halls and service buildings, connected by

31

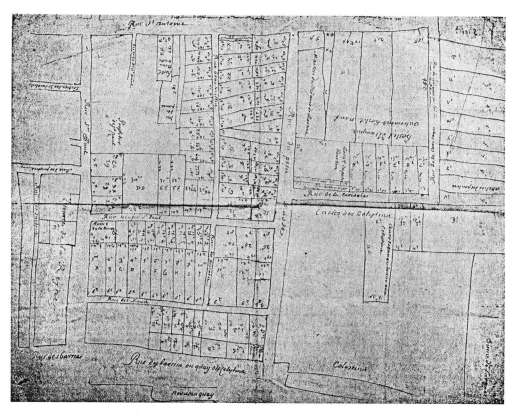

17
Plan of the *lotissement* of the Hôtel Saint-Pol from 1543 to 1556, from Mirot.

galleries and arbours and separated by irregular courtyards and gardens, as was the Hôtel Saint-Pol of Charles V and VI. Parts of these sprawling complexes had been given or leased to royal favourites up to the 1520s, and the resolve of the Crown to generate the maximum revenue from these *lotissements* is shown in the revocation of all gifts and termination of leases on small and large portions of the properties, so that these new *quartiers* could be methodically developed with grid pattern streets and regular building plots to attract those with means. As can be seen in the outline plans of the *lotissements* of the Hôtel de Flandre and the Hôtel Saint-Pol (Figs 16–17) the scale of the plots varies with the smaller lots usually lining those streets which were expected to be the busiest, for houses with shops or offices on the ground floor of a kind seen in du Cerceau's first project (Figs 8–9). The large plots for substantial houses were on the streets which were quieter without direct access between the main thoroughfares.

Encouraged by the example and initiative of the Crown, the prior of the Church of Sainte-Catherine, which stood north-west of the Hôtel Saint-Pol on the north side of the rue Saint-Antoine, resolved to sell for upper-class development the meadows and market gardens north of the church. Saint-

Catherine already drew part of its income from some houses which stood between the church and the rue Saint-Antoine, which from the fourteenth century had been leased for periods of ninety-nine years. By the 1540s the increased number of monks meant that income from existing leases and other sources of revenue was inadequate and they set about exploiting their major asset the Culture Sainte-Catherine. During the first three months of 1545 (new style) the legal formalities of the conditions of sale and lease were decided upon and completed, and the plan of the *lotissement* was drawn up by the prior, a notary and other unidentified professional men,[9] with a scale of prices for leases (Fig. 18). At the south-east a new area was opened at the west end of the church from which started the Grande rue Sainte-Catherine, one of two long streets running from south to north, the other being the shorter rue Payenne named after Payen the monks' notary, and from west to east across the middle of the area an extended rue des Francs Bourgeois. Of the fifty-nine circled numbered plots shown in the outline plan (Fig. 18), fifty-three were sold between March and June 1545, most of which were between 120 and 150 square *toises*. As the outline plan shows, the greater number of lots were bought up in multiples of two to five, and the list of the first buyers and later owners on the Culture Sainte-Catherine is full of the names of leading lords, courtiers, diplomats and administrators. Robert Dallington writing in or shortly after 1598, having described the Tuileries noted, 'There be other very many and stately buildings, as that of Mons. Sansuë, Mons. de Monpensier, de Nevers, and infinite others, whereof especially towardes the East (i.e. the Marais and especially the Culture Sainte-Catherine) and this towne is full, in so much as ye may say of the French Noblesse, as is elsewhere said of the Agrigentines, "They build as if they should live ever, and feede, as if they should die tomorrow". But among all these, there is none (sayth this Author) that exceed more than the Lawyers, "Les gens de Justice (et sur tout les Tresoriers) ont augmenté aux seigneurs l'ardeur de bastir": The Lawyers and especially the Officer's of the King's money, have enflamed in the Nobilitie the desire of building: . . . .'[10]

On 18 March 1545 (new style), only eight days after two notaries had been instructed to 'dresser les baux à rente des terrains', Jacques des Ligneris, seigneur de Crosne and President of the Parlement de Paris exactly the kind of man referred to by Dallington, bought the five plots 27 to 31, a total of 600 *toises*. Des Ligneris built a house on this land which is of central importance in the history of French Renaissance architecture and sculpture, and which in company with documented or surviving houses from the reigns of Henri II, Charles IX and Henri III made the *lotissement* of the Culture Sainte-Catherine the greatest architectural event and opportunity of the period, and a remarkable commercial success for the monks.[11]

The stimulus for the upper classes to build in Paris during the middle and late sixteenth century has been attributed to decisions made by François I. The speed with which the leases on the Culture Sainte-Catherine were

18
Plan of the *lotissement* of the Culture Sainte-Catherine in 1545, from Dumolin.

snapped up proves the strength of the need and demand for building land within the walls of Charles V. Other royal edicts put further pressure on the available land between the two sets of medieval walls, the inner and earlier set of Philippe Auguste and the outer range from the reign of Charles V. Henri II's ordonnance of 23 November 1548 forbade any new building in the *faubourgs* just outside the walls on both banks, and the act was to be enforced by demolition at the owner's expense with other penalties. The ordonnance was renewed on a number of occasions during the later sixteenth and seventeenth centuries because of the problems of policing and servicing an uncontrolled expansion of the city. The royal and municipal jurisdiction might have been extended to areas beyond the walls, but this was not considered to be in the interests of the city's privileges, economy or security.

After the death in 1559 of Henri II from wounds after a jousting accident at the Hôtel des Tournelles, his superstitious widow Catherine de Medici decided to sell the rambling palace. The exact limits of the Tournelles are not easy to follow now, but it was a considerable area on the north side of the rue Saint-Antoine, opposite the Hôtel Saint-Pol, the neighbour of the Culture Sainte-Catherine to the west with the walls of Charles V on the east. Letters patent published on 23 January 1563 describe a programme for the development of the quarter which is the earliest record of a fully coherent royal initiative in town planning.[12] The document starts with the usual preamble on the city daily growing more populous and how the majority of newcomers and natives are obliged to build outside the walls of the city because of the shortage of building space. Philibert de l'Orme's brother Jean was to design a pattern of streets and open spaces; land was to be sold in regular plots on condition that the purchasers built their houses within two years. The novel clause in the text is the proviso on the houses being 'uniformes et semblables'. Jean de l'Orme was to design a comprehensive scheme with architecturally coherent street elevations, but unfortunately the letters patent do not specify whether the intention was to create an *haut-bourgeois* and aristocratic residential quarter or one which incorporated a mixture of commercial premises with housing for a wide social spectrum. Any drawings made by l'Orme for the transformation of the area have not survived and the project was never started, but something of the 1563 scheme may be echoed in the Place des Vosges built forty years later for Henri IV on part of the site of the derelict Hôtel des Tournelles, which determined the east of the Marais as *haut bourgeois* and aristocratic.

Estimates of the size of the population of Paris during the sixteenth century vary, and considerable fluctuations are to be expected with the horrors of the Wars of Religion in the second half of the century. Figures of 350,000 to 500,000 have been given for the late 1520s, with one million in 1577, which drops to 200,000 to 300,000 souls in 1596. The guesses of a Venetian ambassador or a modern historian of the city's population do little to help with the history of the physical development and rate of building expansion of Paris. The periods of pressure of population led to taller tenement building in the older quarters on or near the main arteries, the rue Saint-Denis, the rue Saint-Martin on the Right Bank and the rue Saint-Jacques on the Left Bank. The story of the *lotissements* illustrates one aspect of the filling in of the area within the walls, but this process should not be related to pressures from a growing population, but to the ambitions of speculators, and of the wealthy for a more salubrious life in the town with gardens and other agreeable features. The first large addition to the limits of Paris on the Right Bank since the fourteenth century was the start made in 1566 on new fortifications for the west of the city, and which moved the Porte Saint-Honoré out by 950 metres.[13] Only with the completion of the *fossés jaunes* under Louis XIII, which ran from the west end of the Tuileries gardens round to the Porte Poissonière in the north, did a full and rational *lotissement* of the area take place. The improvement in the city's appearance foreseen by François I in 1543 was not a radical or grandiose proposal to embellish the capital of the kind which preoccupied architects under all of the Bourbon Kings and Napoleon, but it was a practical wish to see accommodated a larger resident professional aristocratic class in new and renewed portions of the Right Bank, and at a profit to the crown.

Once a gentleman or businessman had bought his land on one of the *lotissements*, he was usually obliged as a condition of the sale to build within a prescribed number of years, and one of the results of such stipulations was numerous cases of sale and resale before any building was started. The design of the house might be entrusted to an architect, but from the evidence of the great majority of surviving building contracts, an architect was consulted or employed on surprisingly few occasions in the second half of the century. Custom and architectural books advised the patron to seek competent advice before any commitment by contract to building, on all matters of form and size, materials and their cost, and of course style. Social connections greatly influenced the appearances of some buildings in sixteenth-century France, where groups of amateurs and craftsmen convened to discuss ideal and practical matters,[14] but records of such collaborations do not survive for any Parisian *hôtel* although they must have taken place. Amongst the upper classes were men who had travelled and who had read Vitruvius and other architectural literature, but only rarely is there any trace of their taste, and their impact is impossible to judge.[15] Only in the case of Pierre Lescot, the designer of the Louvre, do we have an exceptional and spectacular case of a courtier prevailing in favour over the specialized architect who, in the early history of the new Louvre, was Sebastiano Serlio.[16] The most common and convenient intermediary for a patron was his notary, the man who for all important contracts drew up the terms to be agreed between patron and master mason, and their growing expertise in the economics of building led to the appointment of notaries to the senior post in the Royal Works under Henri III and Henri IV. The building contract may or may not mention a drawing on which the agreement has been based, and contracts are never good records of the stylistic details of buildings, for they are concerned with type, quality and price of materials, but contracts are invaluable for information about the dispositions of a house, and without them few reconstructions of the plans of lost buildings could be attempted. In such precise and detailed documents as Parisian masonry contracts it is surprising and frustrating to find only the most cursory descriptions of the decorative elements of the projected building, as these would be agreed on the basis of a drawing provided by or on behalf of the patron, and which would be initialled by all the parties to the contract. The loss of the drawings once attached to contracts in the notarial archives is almost total, and so it is from the costings, and the amount of more expensive *toises*, that a notion of the architectural interest of a building can be extracted. These documents almost never specify the particularities of any classical ornament to be made; whether a column or pilaster was to be Doric, Ionic or Corinthian presumably had little bearing on the amount of money involved in a bargain. The notarial building contract gave the patron assurances on the cost of work and on the date on which work would be started. Many contracts only describe a portion of a full scheme foreseen by patron, architect or master mason. The story of sixteenth-century architecture in Paris is full of curious fragments and never completed *hôtels* and judgements on the success or failure of a design should be cautious.

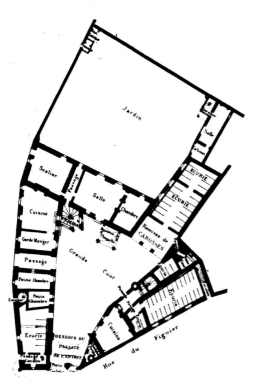

19
Hôtel de Sens. Ground-floor plan with supposed
original dispositions.

20
Hôtel de Sens. Bird's-eye view by Gaignières.

CHAPTER II

Late Gothic and Early Renaissance Houses

Two imposing houses, built by Princes of the Church, survive from the last quarter of the fifteenth century. These are the essential starting point for any discussion of the birth and development of the 'classic' and classical Parisian *hôtel*. The Hôtel des Archevêques de Sens in the east of the old city on the Right Bank was begun in 1475 and was completed by 1507 (Figs 19–23) and the Hôtel des Abbés de Cluny on the Left Bank was begun ten years later and was completed by 1510 (Figs 24–28).[1] Neither is classical, but the comparison and contrast of the two houses show decisive changes in organization which illustrate the act of conception of the 'classic' Parisian town house.

The stern appearance of the Hôtel de Sens is in keeping with our knowledge of the personality of its builder Tristan de Salazar. He was a soldier from his earliest manhood, and entered the church at the age of thirty. As a special mark of favour and gratitude for his father, Jean de Salazar's military service to the Crown, and in particular for a rescue by Jean de Salazar of the King from danger at the Battle of Montlhéry, Louis XI gave the archbishopric of Sens to Tristan de Salazar in 1474 when he was thirty-three. As a warrior and as a diplomat, Tristan de Salazar was a conspicuous figure at the Courts of Charles VIII and Louis XII, and the chroniclers and satirists of the period portray him as an ambitious, ruthless and avaricious man, with, in the words of one text, '. . . a heart open to all evil and closed to all virtue . . .'[2] Salazar was criticized above all by contemporaries for greedily accumulating benefices and for being litigious, for the number of disputes he had with the priesthood at Sens, but Sens Cathedral was repaired and completed with large gifts from him which far exceeded the sums devoted to the building advanced by any of his immediate predecessors. An eighteenth-century guide to Paris[3] records an inscription on the Hôtel de Sens which dated from the builder's time and read 'Tristan, avec un art tout nouveau, releva ce sublime édifice, dont la vétusté consommait la ruine. Si le ciel accorde de longs jours à ce grand homme, sa mémoire sera partout célèbre dans la postérité.' Little can be said to confirm or contradict the boast of the Hôtel de Sens as built 'avec un art tout nouveau' without visual records of other important *hôtels* of the mid and late fifteenth century. The outstanding features of the exterior are the three pepperpot turrets on the main angles of the building, two of which flank the tall pointed arch of the main gate and its attendant pedestrian gateway at the right. If there were openings in the ground floor on the outside, they would have been smaller and fewer than are seen today, with generous transom or mullion and transom windows to light the first and second floors. The outer elevations are crowned by heavily restored dormers on the attic with ogee pediments and fancy pinnacles, and the passerby was further informed of the power and glory of Salazar by a display of heraldry and archbishop's emblems in the tympanum of the main gate, all of which was hacked off during the Revolution, but which is recorded in an eighteenth-century drawing by Gaignières (Fig. 20). The exteriors of the south wing and the surviving portion of the east wing with the gateways are all assymmetrical, but the irregular borders of the site precluded symmetry on the outside where windows were opened where they were needed. The ensemble is given coherence by the horizontal string courses which run right round the building at first- and second-floor levels, and the entrance is given a balance by the twin pepperpot towers set

21
Hôtel de Sens. Entrance.

22
Hôtel de Sens. Stair tower.

23
Hôtel de Sens. South-western corner showing the different floor levels.

at the same height. These angle turrets were equally for prestige and defence. The curious penchant of the bourgeoisie and aristocracy for corner towers and turrets will be discussed below. The Hôtel de Sens is the last known domestic building in Paris to have serious provision made against an attack, not only with the angle turrets on the outside but also inset shoots in the point of the arch of the main gate and in the staircase tower in the courtyard for discharging boiling liquids.

The picturesque irregularity of the outside is partly a result of the shape of the site, but is also an early example of a building designed from the inside out, as commented upon by Serlio, with windows pierced where needed. In contrast, the original surviving parts of the courtyard have straight walls, and the courtyard shape as originally laid out was probably an isosceles triangle with the outer left pier of the main gate as its apex and the court front of the west wing or *corps de logis* as the short side of the figure. Unfortunately the exact length of the west wing is uncertain, and its relationship to and the original dispositions of the wing on the rue Figuier are unknown. The plan of the Hôtel de Sens contains many pointers to future developments with its gateways almost parallel with the *corps de logis* which bisects the site dividing the courtyard from the garden. The *corps de logis* is one room deep allowing views on to the courtyard or garden, and as its length is almost on a north/south axis, the main rooms would be lit by the milder morning and evening light as recommended by custom and later architectural writers.

We shall never know what was meant by the 'art tout nouveau' mentioned in the lost inscription, but the two most notable features of the courtyard as built were the projecting apse of the chapel near to or in the middle of the *corps de logis* and the stair tower, which still exists (Fig. 22). The pedigree of the large spiral projecting staircase is long and varied in French medieval domestic architecture. It gives access to all the floors both major and minor, but most interesting is its location in the Hôtel de Sens at the junction of the *corps de logis* and the apartments of the south wing. Such staircases often served both to give access to each of the floors of wings which might contain different numbers of levels and to act as a partition, allowing floors or wings to be locked off from the public or business activities of the house.

The atmosphere created by the architecture of the Hôtel de Sens is military and grave, and in comparison the Hôtel de Cluny is cheerful. The *hôtel* was built between 1485 and 1498,[4] whilst the beautiful gallery on the left-hand side of the courtyard was added between 1500 and 1510. Jacques d'Amboise was the seventh brother in a generation when the Amboise family were at the zenith of their power and prestige under Louis XII.[5] The youngest of the brothers, Georges, Archbishop of Rouen, was the undisputed power in the land from 1498 to his death in 1510. The patronage of all the arts and architecture by the Amboise outshone that of any other family of the late fifteenth- and the first decade of sixteenth-century France

24
Hôtel de Cluny.
Engravings from Albert
Lenoir's *Statistique
Monumentale de Paris* of
1867.

25
Hôtel de Cluny. Stair tower and eastern portions of the courtyard.

including that of the Crown, in its quantity, variety and modernity, and it
is in the patronage of the Amboise that 'the vital steps towards Italianism'
can be traced,[6] which profoundly influenced royal and aristocratic taste
in painting, sculpture and architecture. At Gaillon from 1502 Georges
d'Amboise rebuilt the castle in the most opulent flamboyant Gothic style

26
Hôtel de Cluny. Gallery.

which was succeeded by a classical style with the arrival of artists from northern Italy in 1508.[7] Gaillon is the acknowledged stylistic watershed in French architectural decoration, but Georges d'Amboise had built in Rouen one of the largest and most spectacular late Gothic domestic buildings,[8] the Palais de Justice (Fig. 29). Beside the Palais de Justice of Rouen or Gaillon, Jacques d'Amboise's Parisian *hôtel* looks modest in scale and in the richness and intricacy of its applied decoration.

According to Pierre de Saint-Julien, in his *Mélanges paradoxalles et receuils de diverses matières pour la pluspart paradoxalles, & neantmoins vrayes . . .*, published at Lyon in 1588, the Hôtel de Cluny and others of Jacques d'Amboise's building works, the repair of the Collège de Cluny close to the *hôtel* and the abbot's house at Cluny, were paid for out of 50,000 *angelots* of booty from the estates of English members of the Order of Cluny. Saint-Julien says this huge sum was accumulated within the space of three years, but adds that this should be thought neither excessive nor strange as the Head of the Order was the traditional beneficiary after the deaths of members of the Order. Such ecclesiastical benefices, notes Saint-Julien, made kings envious.

The main wing of the Hôtel de Cluny would have been built at right angles to the gallery, at the left of the court and the lateral block on the right, had the oblique angle of the street been less pronounced. The slight obtuse angle of the junction of the *corps de logis* and the gallery is not obvious when passing through the gate in the crenellated screen wall to admire the decoration and clever organization of the courtyard elevations. As shown by Albert Lenoir's engravings, the three quarters of the main façade seen when passing through the gate was symmetrical with three window bays widely separated, framed on the left by the gallery and on the right by the projecting octagonal staircase. The entrance to the staircase which leads up to the largest room in the enfilade of the *corps de logis* is carefully aligned with the gate, and also screens the different and concentrated fenestration of the eastern quarter of the main front. The courtyard elevations are devised with what we might call 'local symmetry', with each portion designed to be seen as a complete and coherent, if not an independent composition. With the conversion of the Hôtel de Cluny into a museum during the 1850s two more pairs of windows were pierced in the front between the gallery and the stair tower, and the picturesque asymmetry which the restorers thought of as truly Gothic, has destroyed the careful balance and proportions devised by the anonymous architect of the 1480s.[9] Horizontal string courses run right round the courtyard binding all the portions of the elevation and, in contrast to the Hôtel de Sens, express the equality and consistency of height of the ground and first floors in all the wings. The richest decoration on the *corps de logis* and the right lateral block is reserved for the attic storey with its elaborate cornice covered with vegetable and witty animal and human caricatures, and an ornate balustrade with tall and elaborate sculptured dormers above. The gallery on the left was given special treatment with pointed arches enriched with crocketed blind ogees, and the horizontal with vertical courses which make a dense grid on the first floor. In the dormer of the gallery is the first evidence in Paris of the north Italian classicism imported to Gaillon during these years, with the square pilasters which rise at left and right of the pediment (Fig. 26). The open arcade of the gallery gave shelter for servants and stores, but its main use was as an access to the stable court which was one of the chambers of the Roman baths adjacent.

The organization of the elements in the plan of the Hôtel de Cluny is replete with traditional and forward-looking features. The entrance screen is only a token gesture of defence, and its height was calculated to allow a view from the street of the house's crown of cornice and dormers. The mounted visitor to the Hôtel de Cluny would dismount in the most spacious end of the courtyard with his horse being led away to the left, whilst he or she would walk to the prominent *escalier d'honneur* at the right. Projecting towers for staircases have become a theme for specialized study,[10] and apart from prominence in architectural ensembles they played an important role in the etiquette and ritual of royal and aristocratic houses, for example from the famous Louvre staircase of Charles V[11] to the Hôtel Jacques Coeur at Bourges of 1452 to 1456, the lavish Tour du Lion on the

27
Hôtel de Cluny. Exterior of the chapel.

28
Hôtel de Cluny. Interior of the chapel.

29
The Palais de Justice of Rouen.

Château de Meillant built by Jacques d'Amboise's brother, Charles II d'Amboise, and on to the first building initiative of François I's reign at Blois of 1515 to 1524. Where a host greeted his guest would be decided upon according to the rank of the visitor. On the staircase of the Hôtel de Cluny are the arms and emblems of Jacques d'Amboise (Fig. 25) rather than on the street front chosen by Tristan de Salazar, and it gives access to ground, first and attic floors. It is not possible to be certain that the first floor contained the fine reception rooms and the private rooms of Jacques d'Amboise, but with the chapel and gallery at this level, this floor was surely the *piano nobile*, with the ground floor for guest rooms and offices, with service functions in the ground floor of the right lateral block. The staircase of the house was carefully placed on the façade to give access, but also to mark a partition between the public and private areas of the building, and on this principle, seen in other houses, all the rooms to the right of the *escalier d'honneur* should have been private apartments.

The chapel of the Hôtel de Cluny is the only feature of the interior to survive, although even it is not intact. In plan, the chapel is almost square, with a central pillar supporting elaborate flamboyant rib vaults (Fig 28). In the upper tier of the walls are intricately carved canopied niches where there were statues of members of the Amboise family instead of saints or martyrs, but private chapels or family chapels in churches were often used

49

to express dynastic pride with inscriptions, paintings or sculpture.[12] Cardinal's hats decorated the walls above the doors of the enfilade of the *corps de logis*, and as completed for Jacques d'Amboise the house must have been as full of family imagery inside, as outside. The wealth and taste of the Amboise are displayed unequivocally in the Hôtel de Cluny but it did not remain with the family as it was built for the Order, and was leased by them from Jacques d'Amboise's death in 1516 up to the Revolution, and provided a healthy income. The Venetian ambassador reported in 1577 that '. . . [Parisian *hôtels*] are almost always rented furnished, by the day or by the month; for the concierges whom we might call the estate agents for houses and palaces, find it unwise to do otherwise for fear of their master's sudden return to Court. When that happens one has to decamp quickly, above all when it is the house of a great lord. This has happened during my own time here to the Papal Nuncio Salviati, who was forced to move three times within the space of two months.' The Hôtel de Cluny had more considerate landlords for a long line of illustrious lessees beginning with Louis XII's widow Mary of England, and it was here in the next century that Mazarin first stayed in the French capital.

Only a small group of interesting buildings are recorded and can be described from the reign of Louis XII (1498 to 1515) but each of this group of two or possibly three buildings is of exceptional quality, the Hôtel le Gendre, enlarged and embellished around 1506 on the rue des Bourdonnais to the north-east of the Louvre in the 'quartier des Halles' (Figs 30–37), the Chambre des Comptes begun in 1504 which stood beside the Sainte-Chapelle on the Ile de la Cité (Fig. 38), and to these two might be added the mysterious and undatable Hôtel des Ursins which was once a landmark of the north side of the Ile de la Cité opposite the place de Grève and the Hôtel de Ville (Figs 40–43).

The demolition of the Hôtel le Gendre in 1841 might have obliterated all trace of a special building in the history of Parisian architecture, but the announcement of its imminent destruction provoked a fervent outcry from architects and antiquarians led by Viollet-le-Duc, which did not succeed in saving the building, but led to many of its decorative elements being preserved, and to reconstructions of its original appearance being made.[13] Romantic lithographers as much as antiquarians admired the jaded opulence of the house, but Viollet-le-Duc and Albert Lenoir studied the building, to publish reconstructions which remain the most vivid record of a lost masterpiece. Records of the Hôtel le Gendre are of exceptional value and significance because it is the last important *hôtel* whose plan and whose elevations are known and can be studied in detail, before a gap in our knowledge which extends to the mid 1540s. At least a quarter of a century of Paris' domestic architecture remains obscure, with only a small number of interesting buildings known from seventeenth- and eighteenth-century plans.

Pierre le Gendre (*c.* 1465–1524) was one of four 'Trésoriers de France'

30
Hôtel Le Gendre. View of the north side of the courtyard about 1840.

and a rich and well-connected royal servant. The inventory of the contents of his house in the rue des Bourdonnais and of his country properties covers 491 folios which list about 2,250 objects, and is a valuable social document which describes the use of each room of the house and their fittings and furniture.[14] The list of the contents of the Hôtel le Gendre covers 250 folios with descriptions and valuations of every item from expensive furniture and tapestries, wall hangings, works of art and arms, to small utilitarian items in the kitchen and stables. This inventory provides detailed proof of the role of the staircase as a means of access and of partition. Pierre le Gendre built his house both as a home and as a work place with, on a floor level below the first leg of the gallery which connects with the entrance wing, (Fig. 35), the 'comptouer des clercs' or bank for his administration and secretaries.[15] Viollet-le-Duc's plan shows no direct passage from this office to the main block other than across the stairs, and as seen in Pugin's beautiful drawing of the interior (Fig. 36), the door which led into the 'comptouer des clercs' was not on the same level as any of the floors of the main block. People with business at the house might only glimpse the door of the private apartments up another flight of the spiral from the offices.

At the time of his death le Gendre's house was packed with furniture, tapestries and objets d'art, especially the apartments of the ground and first floors of the *corps de logis* which were replete with luxury goods of all

51

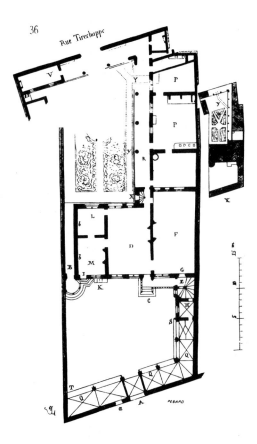

31
Hôtel Le Gendre. Plan from Viollet Le Duc's
Dictionnaire de l'Architecture, tome VI.

kinds. The inventory lists numerous oak chests and caskets dispersed around the house, for the regal quantities of his clothes and other valuables. The first-floor gallery which ran from above the bank to a chapel at the far end of the entrance wing was the only part of the house left sparsely furnished with a solitary settle.[16] Seventeenth- and eighteenth-century texts on the running of households insisted on the master's obligation to see that his servants celebrated mass twice daily. The bareness of this portion of the Hôtel le Gendre suggests that the chapel in the entrance wings was for communal use, and le Gendre might have had a private oratory in the *tourelle* (Fig. 37).

If the inventory of the Hôtel le Gendre had not survived, most of the domestic arrangements could have been divined from the plan, with the master's quarters in the middle of the site overlooking the forecourt and the garden, and having the kitchens and stables at the end of the garden with a service gate on to the rue Tirechappe. The contrast between the austerity of the street front (Fig. 32) and the opulence of the courtyard fronts made the passage from the outside the more impressive, as can still be experienced at the Hôtel de Cluny walking through the entrance screen. The gateway on to the rue des Bourdonnais was framed by a bizarre com-

32
Hôtel Le Gendre. Street front on the rue des Bourdonnais, from Albert Lenoir's *Statistique Monumentale de Paris* of 1867.

33
Hôtel Le Gendre. Courtyard side of the entrance front from Albert Lenoir's *Statistique Monumentale de Paris* of 1867.

34
Hôtel Le Gendre. Courtyard elevation of the *corps de logis* as reconstructed by Viollet Le Duc in his *Dictionnaire de l'Architecture*, tome VI.

35
Hôtel Le Gendre. Elevation of the north wing linking the *corps de logis* with the entrance wing, as reconstructed for Albert Lenoir's *Statistique Monumentale de Paris* of 1867.

36
Hôtel Le Gendre. Interior view of the staircase dividing the *corps de logis* from the north wing, drawing by Pugin.

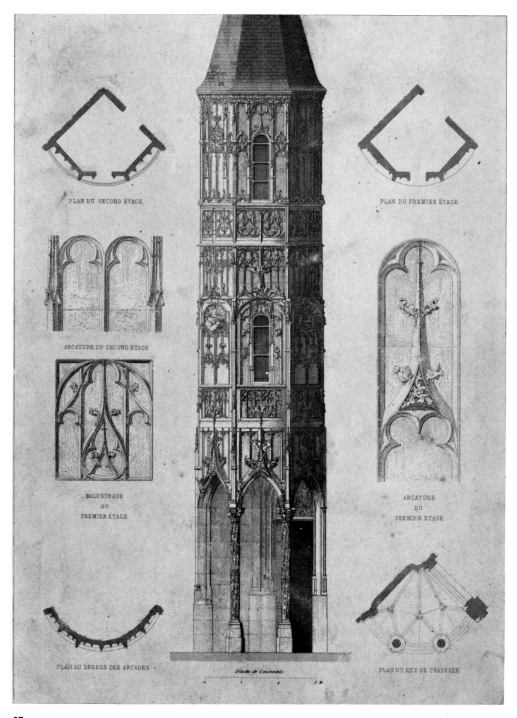

37
Hôtel Le Gendre. Elevation and details of the *tourelle* in the left-hand corner of the courtyard, from Albert Lenoir's *Statistique Monumentale de Paris* of 1867.

position of raised pilasters and with a triangular arrangement of acanthus branches which faintly resemble a pediment. With its historical or portrait medallions and pilasters the entrance of the Hôtel le Gendre is the earliest truly Italianate piece of decorative design recorded in Paris, but it is more in keeping with the kind of design found on the title page of a book than with contemporary or near contemporary architecture in northern Italy or Rome.[17] The courtyard in its original condition was a showcase for the range and diversity of the skill of the Parisian master mason with decorative tracery.

Each of the six horizontal decorative layers of the *tourelle* (Fig. 37) has its own distinctive tracery patterns of varying complexity, with the small tiers between the floor levels and the bottom of the windows having the most intricate and dense compositions, as if they were true screens or balustrades. On the first leg of the gallery (Fig. 35) the three bays have different traceries in the horizontal band dividing the ground and first floors, and only in the dormer pediments, as reconstructed by Lenoir, is there any repetition of a pattern. Unfortunately nothing is known of the garden front; the reconstructions of portions of the courtyard published by Albert Lenoir are meticulous but are not wholly reliable when compared with the surviving fragments, and his conjectures on the roof lines and dormer pediments are reasonable and now cannot be disproved or corrected. The finesse and variety of the Hôtel le Gendre's tracery is one illustration of the vigour and inventiveness of the flamboyant Gothic style in early sixteenth-century France,[18] and with workmanship of such quality it is possible to understand how the fashion for classical decoration was slowed in Paris and the Ile de France.

The Hôtel le Gendre was not a classical house in style, but the dispositions and use of the site are those of a fully evolved 'classic' Parisian town-house plan. Many of the features described by Corrozet in his ideal house were on show at the Hôtel le Gendre with its large entrance gateway, its forecourt with rich decoration and medallions, and the siting of the *corps de logis* in the middle of the site facing one way on to the courtyard and the other on to a pleasant garden, which may have had the sets of antique and modern statuary imagined by Corrozet. The site of the house was long but it was not narrow with a street frontage of just under twenty-five metres in width, and allowed for a spacious court and garden. The Hôtel le Gendre was not planned to make full use of the ground as can be seen with the forecourt which was made as large as possible, the entrance and bank wings were shallow in depth and a wing was not built on the left-hand side to complete the courtyard. In houses where space was limited, kitchens would be housed in the basement of a lateral wing of the *corps de logis*, and horses might be stabled in the vicinity. Le Gendre had built a comprehensive set of service buildings for kitchens, stables and servants' quarters, and judging from the quantities of kitchen equipment listed in the inventory, he could have entertained lavishly in his splendid house.

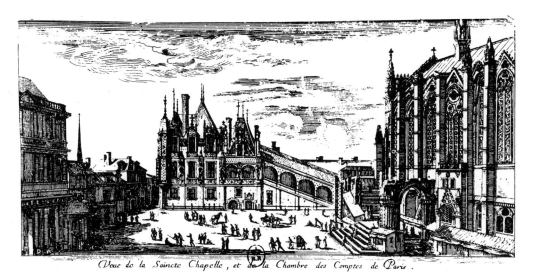

Veue de la Saincte Chapelle, et de la Chambre des Comptes de Paris.

38
The Chambre des Comptes. Engraving by Israel Sylvestre.

The rue des Bourdonnais was amongst the most prestigious streets in the capital in the fifteenth and early sixteenth centuries, as the rue de Grenelle and the rue de Varenne in the faubourg Saint-Germain were to become the addresses of the richest and royal in the eighteenth century. The Hôtel le Gendre had for neighbours the Hôtel de la Trémouïlle on its south side, and to the north the *hôtel* of Louis de Poncher, who was one of the four 'Trésoriers de France' with Pierre le Gendre. It is not possible to estimate whether the Hôtel le Gendre was stylistically advanced or conventional for Paris in the late 1500s, for we know nothing of the style of the houses of le Gendre's peers such as Louis de Poncher, but there can be no doubt that it was designed to impress with its opulence inside and outside, a true 'Invention Joyeuse' in the spirit of Corrozet, for whom the Gothic style was the modern style in his trio of 'Romanesque, Greek and Modern'.

The Chambre des Comptes built in 1504 is the first of a long series, which extends to the late nineteenth century, of government and municipal buildings on whose façades rich ornament and statuary celebrate an institution's standing and historical and moral traditions to the public (Fig. 38). The dormers and the projecting angle turret were covered with intricate carving, and the royal and moral kudos of the Chambre des Comptes was celebrated by the set of five statues in the niches on the first floor which showed Louis XII in company with the four Cardinal Virtues, Temperance, Prudence, Justice and Fortitude. The long arcaded-staircase ramp was used for processions and ceremonies including royal proclamations. The building was burnt out and demolished in 1737, and none of the decorations or sculpture was retained to give us a clearer idea of its style and quality than can be gleaned from Israel Sylvestre's engraving.

39

The Place de Grève and the Ile de la Cité, showing the Hôtel des Ursins at the right of the cross's shaft. Engraving by Israel Sylvestre.

The Ile de la Cité saw very little private residential building during the sixteenth century.[19] The densely populated central section and northern side of the island, with its thirteen parishes and twenty-one places of worship,[20] had become one of the artisan and bourgeois quarters of the city before the mid fifteenth century. The sector in which stood the Hôtel des Ursins was the most notorious enclave, in and around the rue Glatigny which was popularly known as the 'Val d'Amour' with its brothels and taverns[21] (Fig. 39). This tower house is certainly fourteenth century in date and was owned if not built by a famous 'Prévôt des Marchands' Jean Jouvenal des Ursins (1360–1431).[22] Albert Lenoir's reconstruction of the house seen from the river is full of questionable details and is little more than a romantic evocation of a prominent feature of the cityscape, which disappeared about 1769, seen in Sylvestre's engraving (Figs 39–40) and in every painting showing the north side of the Ile de la Cité of the sixteenth to eighteenth centuries in the Musée Carnavalet.[23] The sixteenth- and seventeeth-century paintings agree in showing a tall square tower with full height round-angle turrets, but the paintings show an arcaded loggia below the roof that would have been an early sixteenth-century addition in the style of the terrace arcades shown by Lenoir and in survey drawings of 1760 in the Archives Nationales (Figs 41–43). The top two floors seen in Lenoir's vignette could be the result of a mutilation of the elevation in the eighteenth century, for the house is known to have been split up for multiple occupancy by the mid eighteenth century.

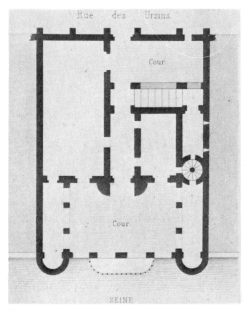

40
Hôtel des Ursins. Reconstruction engravings from Albert Lenoir's *Statistique Monumentale de Paris* of 1867.

The date of the architecture of the terrace cannot be fixed, but the detail of a spandrel from the arcade facing the river published by Lenoir shows that it was in an unadulterated Italian style, unlike any French building of the first half of the sixteenth century. The case for the terrace arcades of the Hôtel des Ursins being an early and direct import, dating no later than 1520, is supported by the character of the medallion shown by Lenoir which resembles those of the Hôtel le Gendre. A shallow cutting into the

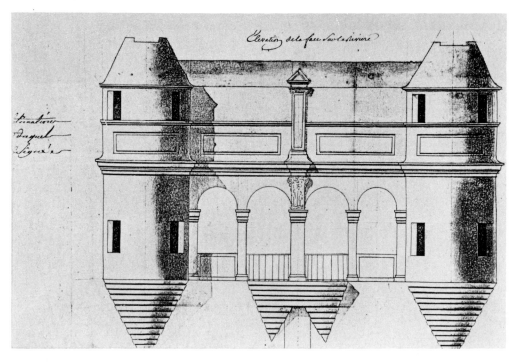

41
Hôtel des Ursins. Terrace front, an eighteenth-century survey drawing.

spandrels left a continuous moulding around the arches which is used to express a key stone at the top of each arch. The clarity and elegance of these Doric arcades made a strange contrast to the solid defensive corner turrets from an earlier building phase, and to the keep which would have excluded sunlight from the terrace. Without an exact dating for the terrace arcades, it is not possible to say which of the early sixteenth-century owners of the house was responsible for this precocious stylistic alteration. The addition of the suffix 'des Ursins' to the family name of Jouvenal came about in the early fifteenth century as a deliberate and bogus attempt to link the Jouvenals with one of the oldest families of Rome, the Orsini.[24] The pure Italian terrace might be the result of a member of the family celebrating this claim in architectural form more than a hundred years after these pretensions are first recorded. The Italian coat of arms depicted by Lenoir in one of the spandrels is not an Orsini coat of arms, but more closely resembles the arms of the noble Venetian family of Foscarini, but this heraldic signature on the building has not been deciphered. From before the beginning of the seventeenth century the Hôtel des Ursins was in decline, or 'in the hands of others' to use Corrozet's phrase, and only one event of interest took place there on the 30 May 1677 when Racine, who had lodgings in the building, agreed on the terms of his marriage contract.[25]

42
Hôtel des Ursins. Section of the terrace, an eighteenth-century survey drawing.

The reign of François I from 1515 to 1547 was a great age of country house building in the Loire Valley during its first half, and in the Ile de France during the second half, and the story of developments in classical styles under François I has to be told using examples from provincial cities and of country houses.

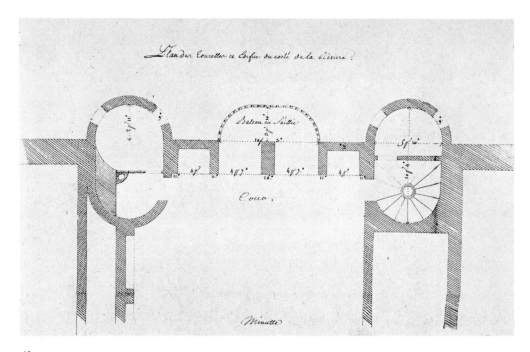

43
Hôtel des Ursins. Plan of the terrace, an eighteenth-century survey drawing.

The transition from the flamboyant Gothic style to the fashion for classical motifs can be illustrated by the decoration of angle turrets, in which Paris was once rich but now is poor.[26] These expensive appendages, which required specialized knowledge of geometry in a master mason, were in medieval times considered as symbols of status for a monarch only,[27] but by the sixteenth century the affluent were seeking permission from the Parlement de Paris to add angle turrets to their houses as public statements of their civic and personal pride. The turret of the Hôtel Jean d'Hérouet is the only survivor in a Gothic style, and is thought to date from the reign of Louis XII,[28] (Fig 44), and like that of the Chambre des Comptes (Fig 38) spans two storeys and is octagonal. The elaborate blind tracery on this middle-sized private house can only be compared to the Hôtel le Gendre, where on the courtyard *tourelle* the patterning was more intricate. It has been claimed that the Renaissance was the only architectural revolution which did not bring with it any technical changes or reforms.[29] The idea has its faults, but on Parisian angle turrets, whether round, square or octagonal, a variety of Italianate detail displaced the Gothic and produced some curious effects without any innovations in engineering. The proportions of a correctly-drawn pilaster were not suited to a tall narrow angle-turret, and the resulting distortions can be seen in two lost examples on the rue des Prêtes Saint-Germain l'Auxerrois (Fig. 45 top left) and on the rue de la Mortellerie (Fig 45 bottom centre) both of

44
Hôtel d'Herouet. Present condition.

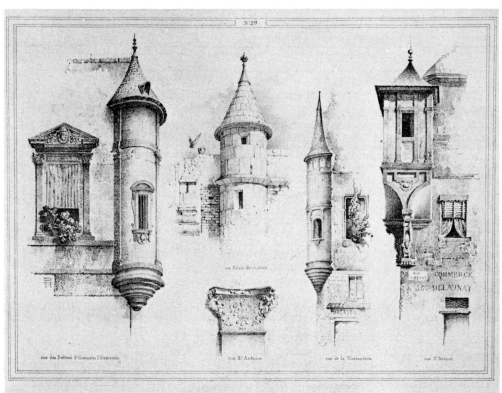

rue des Prêtres St Germain l'Auxerrois.   au Palais de Justice.   rue St Antoine.   rue de la Tixeranderie.   rue St Benoît.

Rue de la Mortellerie.

66

45
Corner turrets of the fifteenth to seventeenth
centuries, from L. T. Turpin De Crissé's *Souvenirs
du Vieux Paris* of 1836.

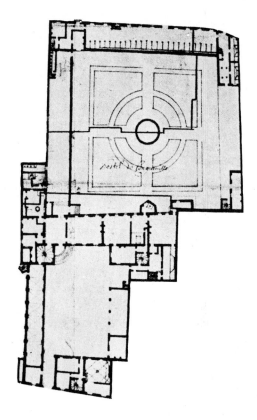

46
Hôtel de Neufville
Villeroy, rue des Poulies.
Seventeenth-century plan.

which must have dated from the early years of François I. The corner turret
of the Hôtel des Abbés de Fécamp survives (Fig. 45 bottom left) and was
once decorated with royal lilies and salamander of François I,[30] but here no
attempt was made on the elongated surfaces to graft classical detail. Inside,
this turret there was in Lenoir's day magnificent inlaid panelling, and such
luxurious fittings show that a feature which was originally for a house's
defence, a place from which to watch the street, had become a place for
privacy and comfort.[31] These sanctums, like an Italian 'studiolo', might
have been the only truly private place for the master of a busy household.
Jean de Vignolles, a notary and Royal secretary, applied to the Parlement
de Paris in 1533 for permission to build a projecting angle turret on his
house at the corner of the rue Saint-Denis and the Aubry-le-Boucher
opposite the future Fontaine des Innocents, and he described his proposal
in patriotic terms, '. . . une tourelle triomphant, à l'antique, ymagée du roy
et autres images, à la grande décoration et honnesté de la ville', for which
permission was granted.[32]

Pierre le Gendre died without children, and his fortune passed to the
Neufville Villeroy family,[33] which provided three generations of secretaries of state to the Valois Kings.[34] Le Gendre's beneficiary was his
nephew, Nicolas I de Neufville-Villeroy, who had built a spacious house

within the dense 'quartier des Halles' on the rue des Poulies, on which building was begun before 1520 and continued throughout the reign of François I.[35] Nothing is known of the Hôtel de Neufville-Villeroy's elevations, but the plan alone is of outstanding importance in the sparse architectural history of Paris before the 1540s (Fig. 46). From the late seventeenth-century plan, where the house appears as the 'Hôtel de Longueville', the 'hôtel' appears with all its later additions, but the enfilade of the main block and the arcaded gallery at right angles to it on the left of the courtyard are amongst the original portions. The mentality behind the planning of the Hôtel Neufville-Villeroy amplified and regularized the pattern set at the Hôtel de Cluny and modified for a smaller scale for Pierre le Gendre. The main staircase was the spiral in the square angle-pavilion in the left of the court, from which there was access to all levels of the main block and to the gallery, but which at ground-floor level, shown by the plan, partitioned off the agglomerate of the ancillary buildings behind. The site was irregular, but the main block was placed almost half way down the plot, beyond which was the broader regular expanse of the garden. This plan shows the *hôtel* in an expanded form, and we cannot be sure of the original arrangements made for stabling horses, whether they sheltered at the right-hand side of the courtyard, or at the end of the garden as at the Hôtel le Gendre, where in the late seventeenth century there were stalls for twenty-five horses, a considerable number in a town house. Our ignorance of the appearance of this house is the more unfortunate, because de Neufville was closely involved with Italian and French artists and architects during the late 1520s and 1530s in his role as superintendent of the works at the Château de Madrid in the Bois de Boulogne.[36]

The variety of classical styles current in Paris before the upsurge of building during the 1540s can be seen in engravings recording a house on the rue Saint-Paul, the Hôtel Tyson and the imposing Hôtel d'Etampes (Figs 47–49) none of which can be accurately dated, and whose building histories are unknown. The curious hybrid decoration of candelabra pilasters, medallions and vegetable motifs of the house on the rue Saint-Paul, is a kind of ornament more usually found on furniture and on altarpiece frames.[37] Few buildings of this size or style are known, but it is comparable in scale and in many details of its decoration to a house built by Nicolas Chabouillé at Moret, which is dated to the years 1515–1525.[38] If the house on the rue Saint-Paul was as early as 1525, it predates the major transformation of the area in which it stood, the *lotissement* of the Hôtel Saint-Pol. The Hôtel Tyson in the 'quartier des Halles' was built shortly before 1531[39] and is curious in having Gothic decoration on its angle turret (Fig. 45 bottom right) and Renaissance decoration on the main body of the house, the most elaborate relief work being reserved for the dormers (Fig. 48). This substantial house is the only known Parisian example of the use of the old and the new style together, but there must have been others.

The Hôtel d'Etampes stood in a prominent position on the Left Bank

47
House, 27 rue Saint-Paul. Reconstruction engraving of 1870, and a surviving detail.

48
Hôtel Tyson. Engraving of its condition in 1830 by Martial Potémont.

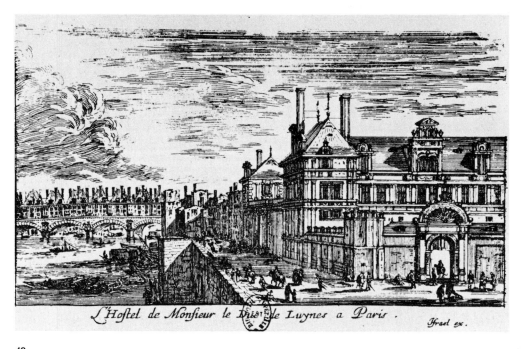

L'Hoftel de Monfieur le Duc de Luynes a Paris.   Ifrael ex.

49
Hôtel d'Etampes (later de Luynes). View from the west by Israel Sylvestre.

opposite the Ile de la Cité just west of the Pont Notre-Dame (Fig. 49). It was demolished about 1670, and no early documents concerning it have been found in the archives, no plan has come to light, and only one partial view of it from a distance shows its elaborate classical elevations.[40] François I's most enduring mistress, Anne Pisseleu, Duchesse d'Etampes, might have commissioned the design of the building, but it was built on a site given by the King and certainly with monies from his purse, for she was both 'la plus belle des savantes, et la plus savante des belles' and avaricious.[41] The engraving shows a long *corps de logis* with an angle pavilion facing a walled courtyard entered by a monumental pilastered and pedimented gateway. The shell in the curved pediment might have been intended as a symbol of Venus, an amusing landmark announcing the residence of the most favoured Royal mistress.[42] A plan would show the extent of an exceptionally large house and might make possible a reconstruction drawing as has been done for a group of later lost or mutilated *hôtels*. The engraving shows two pavilions on the quayside connected by a tall screen wall, behind which must have been a second courtyard. It would be interesting to know if the second court was the main court, or whether the furthest angle pavilion was built to make a symmetrical composition of the river front, and abutted on to service buildings or stables, rather than a wing of the scale of that shown in the engraving. If the engraving is reliable, the Hôtel d'Etampes had a plain dressed stone-ground floor, separated from the first floor by a wide frieze. The *piano nobile* had an architecture of twin pilasters reminiscent of the François I wing at Blois, with a single pilaster at the middle below an imposing central dormer, an example of the 'concordant disharmony' in fenestration which appealed to Serlio in French domestic architecture of the 1540s and before. The prolific pasticheur Androuet du Cerceau's scheme XXII from his first *Livre d'Architecture* of 1559 (Fig. 14) does not have applied architectural ornament closely resembling that of the Hôtel d'Etampes shown in the engraving, but his project's scale and form make the comparison interesting. A long building one room deep with a central staircase, an enfilade leading from either side of the stairs suitable for an arrangement of presence chambers, antechamber and private apartments in the pavilions, is the plan of a house for a great personage familiar from the mid sixteenth century onwards all over northern Europe.[43]

The Hôtel d'Etampes was probably built during the 1530s under royal auspices, and would have been designed in whole or in part by a senior figure in the Royal Works from one or other of the dynasties of master masons like the Le Bretons or the Chambiges. It is possible that it should have been considered in the next chapter on 'Royal Building' where there is nothing to discuss between the proclamation of 1528 and the appointment of Lescot as architect for the Louvre in 1546.

50
Terraces on the Pont Notre-Dame. Engraving by Marot.

CHAPTER III

Municipal and Royal Building
up to 1559

François I encouraged the building of and contributed money for the new Hôtel de Ville as a practical gesture of his interest and need for a closer relationship with the richest city of his kingdom. The Hôtel de Ville was the most prominent of the municipality's building projects, but the *échevins* were responsible for two interesting developments in town planning leading to and on the Ile de la Cité, the terraced houses on the new Pont Notre-Dame of *c.* 1508 to 1512, and a row of houses which stood between the Petit Pont and the Hôtel Dieu of 1552–1554 (Figs 50–52). Their patronage of the arts in general remains to be studied, but as paymasters for the official royal entries, with their temporary architectural set-pieces of triumphal arches, fountains and perspectives, they provided occasions and opportunities for stylistic innovations from the leading architects and sculptors.

The history of urbanism in Paris conventionally begins with the initiatives of Henri IV during the first decade of the seventeenth century, the building of the place des Vosges begun in 1605, the completion of the Pont Neuf with the triangular place Dauphine at its middle on the western end of the Ile de la Cité and the opening of the rue Dauphine from the south of the bridge, as well as the projected semicircular place de France with its radiating streets in the north-east of the city planned in 1610 but abandoned with the assassination of the King in that year.[1] Henri IV and his minister Sully had a keen interest in improving key vacant portions of the city with terraced houses for upper bourgeois and aristocratic pockets, built efficiently and economically in brick and stone. The example of the cities of Flanders was studied for the organization of publicly-funded urban projects and persuaded the King and his minister of the advantages of brick over the traditional range of stone used in Paris.[2] A hundred years earlier the same considerations faced the council having almost completed the costly replacement of the Pont Notre-Dame, and as finished in 1512 the road over the bridge was flanked by two terraces of gabled houses built of brick and stone at the front, but with cheaper timber framed backs[3] (Figs 50–51). The thirty-four houses in each row consisted of a cellar, a shop with a narrow stair passage at the right leading up to two floors of accommodation one room wide, and an attic under the gable. The luxury trades like shops on main thoroughfares, and the municipality's speculative building on the Pont Notre-Dame attracted good rents from goldsmiths

73

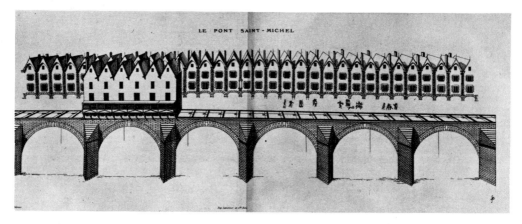

51
The Pont Notre-Dame, described as the Pont Saint Michel. Engraving by Androuet du Cerceau.

52
Terrace between the Petit Pont and the Hôtel Dieu on the south side of the Ile de la Cité. Engraving by Androuet du Cerceau.

and hat makers, and the best known representation of one of these shops on the Pont Notre-Dame is Watteau's painting of Gersaint's *The Picture Dealer,* with its fashionable clientele as much on view to the passerby as the paintings. In early sixteenth-century Paris this type of tall, narrow house was common on the main arteries, but it was the uniformity of the houses on the Pont Notre-Dame which excited contemporaries' admiration,[4] and this uniformity was protected by the council who forbade any alterations by tenants. The lightness of the houses' structures was in part influenced by the need not to make the bridge unstable with a heavy superstructure but, equally important, was economy and the speed of building.

Single-bay terraced houses with an arcade of shops was the formula for the only other municipal speculative development whose appearance is known from one rare engraving (Fig. 52). The builder was the city's master mason, Guillaume Guillain, whose design was vetted carefully or casually by a panel of experts, which included the designer of the Louvre, Pierre Lescot, in 1552.[5] As with the terraces of the Pont Notre-Dame, the two floors of apartments were reached by a passage and stairs to the side of the shop. The principal structural difference is the change from roof gables to a continuous pitched roof. The bond of monarch with his capital is celebrated by the pairs of royal arms in the centre with those of the City of Paris over to the left and right, and to please Henri II further are the emblems of Diana, the bows and crescents over the second-floor windows in tribute to his mistress Diane de Poitiers. The only truly classical features were in the ground-floor arcade with its pillars, block capitals, key stones, oval oculii and triangular pediments over the doors. Above, the windows of the two main floors have mouldings with ears or lugs breaking out at the top sides, which are simplifications of those designed by Lescot for the ground floor of the Louvre. It was natural for a body whose roots were in the merchant guilds to build economical and practical premises for trades, rather than involve itself in residential developments of the more prestigious and risky kind. Their obligations in the sphere of building were with building and maintaining bridges and quaysides, the maintenance and improvement of roads and fountains, the enforcement of building standards and by-laws, rather than with any truly urbanistic notions of the architectural renovation of a quarter of the city as a whole.

The early history of the new Hôtel de Ville is incomplete, especially the circumstances and conditions under which this curious building was designed. In comparison with the cities of Flanders and northern France or the major towns on the Loire, the municipality of Paris had no inspiring institutional building, and as a direct result of the royal declaration of 1528 the *échevins* felt obliged to build premises appropriate for civic and for national occasions. At a meeting on the 29 November 1529 the 'Bureau de la Ville' told the Governor of Paris of their intention to build, and the King promptly assured them of funds.[6]

Designed in 1530 or 1531 by the King's nominee Domenico da Cortona nicknamed the 'Boccador', an Italian long established in France,[7] and executed by the city's master mason Pierre Chambiges,[8] the Hôtel de Ville looks like no Italian building but in its decorative details was the most important Italianate or classical building in the capital before it was eclipsed by the new Louvre. Even with the acquisition of more houses to enlarge the site the planning of the Hôtel de Ville proved awkward, the front facing the place de Grève was the longest side of an irregular trapezoidal courtyard building (Fig. 53). The archway on the right gave access to the rue du Martroi, and to make the façade symmetrical a pair to it was built on the left side which screened the chapel of the Hôpital du Saint Esprit much to the chagrin of the masters and governor of the hospital.[9] Attached Corinthian columns articulated the ground-floor arcade and their tall podia

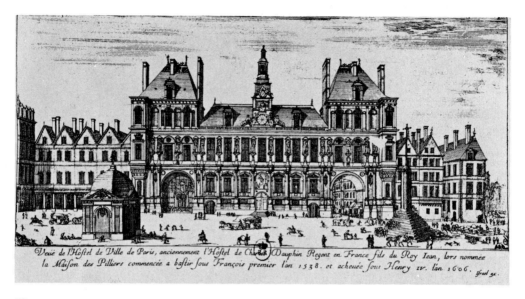

Veuë de l'Hoſtel de Ville de Paris, anciennement l'Hoſtel de Charles Dauphin Regent en France fils du Roy Iean, lors nommée la Maiſon des Pilliers commencée a baſtir ſous François premier l'an 1538. et acheuée ſous Henry IV. l'an 1606. Iſrael ſc.

53
The Hôtel de Ville. Engraving by Israel Sylvestre.

on a blank frieze defined the height of a high basement. Between the two large archways, the ground-floor arcade with its recessed pedimented windows is a revision of the elegant tiers of open arcades of François I's Château de Madrid in the Bois de Boulogne begun in 1528. Correctly, no order stands above the Corinthian of the ground floors, and niches with statues filled the spaces of the main floor, but this may not have been the first architect's intention for the central section of the main floor and the left-hand pavilion above the archway were only completed under Henri IV. The Hôtel de Ville is an intriguing mixture of imported decorative features applied to a building wholly French in form. The silhouette with tall pitched roofs on the three-storey north and south pavilions and the separate pitched roof for the lower main body of the building is a hallmark of the François I style. During the late seventeenth century, when fashion had roofs lowered behind balustrades to make an uninterruped skyline, the new kind of roof was called a 'combe à l'italien'. There is little evidence from sixteenth-century France of new classical decorative styles developing into an interest in all aspects of ancient and contemporary Italian building practice. Indeed, the circumstantial evidence and French architectural pattern books point to a qualified interest in Italian building, where the specialized and virtuoso skills of Parisian master masons and carpenters, in features such as suspended angle turrets and pitched roofs, retained their place in the design of a prestigious building.[10] The two-storey projecting turrets of the Hôtel de Ville, with their springings decorated with layers of motifs adapted from the mouldings of a classical pediment, are proof of the continuity of a building tradition unaffected by

76

54
The Fontaine des Innocents. Engraving by Perelle.

a change in decorative taste. After several interruptions, work stopped on the Hôtel de Ville in 1551, the year in which Pierre Lescot concluded the second and definitive contract for the new Louvre. Lescot was the architect of the Fontaine des Innocents, the most opulent sixteenth-century Parisian water source.

Built on a corner of the rue Saint-Denis the traditional route for royal entries, the Fontaine des Innocents (Fig. 54) was almost complete at the time of Henri II's entry in June 1549.[11] In its present rebuilt state, it is the only vestige of a state entry from the *ancien régime* whose set pieces were usually of wood and canvas, but it is characteristic of the council to make a royal tribute out of a public utility. The basement of the Fontaine des Innocents was the cistern, and its superstructure was wholly ornamental. The motif of the triumphal arch is used in a novel way in being repeated, with two on the long side on the rue aux Fers (now rue Berger) and one on the short side facing the rue Saint-Denis. Between the building of the Hôtel de Ville and the Fontaine des Innocents, illustrated architectural books of ancient and modern design had begun to appear, notably most of Serlio's *libri* amongst which he illustrated a selection of ancient triumphal arches inaccurately. In his designs of arcades and gateways, Serlio distinguished two contrasting manners, the 'rustic' or the bold and massive and the

55
The Fontaine des Innocents. Reliefs by Jean Goujon.

'delicate'.[12] Lescot's arch compositions are elaborate and elegant revisions of the arches he saw in Serlio, with fluted pilasters instead of columns. The partnership of Pierre Lescot with the sculptor Jean Goujon will be described in more detail at the Louvre, but the close incorporation of architectural members with shallow relief sculpture (Fig. 55) guided Lescot towards a composition of fine line which would work well as a framework and a foil for the sculpture. The open loggia was one of the choice viewpoints for the processions of royal entries where a select group of ladies and gentlemen greeted the King. In July 1665 Bernini commented that in his opinion the Fontaine des Innocents was the most beautiful building in Paris,[13] and it is strange that his admiration did not extend to the architecture or sculpture of the Louvre.

As was to be expected, contemporary writing about Lescot and his design of the Louvre are laudatory to the point of being wholly uncritical. The lavish praise of Ronsard's *Elegie à Pierre Lescot* usually finds a place in anthologies of sixteenth-century French verse, and Jacques Androuet du Cerceau properly put the Louvre at the beginning of his two volumes of *Les plus excellents Bastiments de France* in 1576. Only the antiquarian and polymath Blaise de Vigenère felt Lescot's Louvre was too full of mistakes to please the trained eye. During the 1580s he wrote

'Feu Monsieur de Clagny (Pierre Lescot) envers nous, lequel ne s'estant jamais exercé qu'au crayon, plustost encore d'un instinct naturel propre en luy et incliné à la pourtraicture (drawing) que par art acquise, a neantmois conduit assez heureusement le Louvre de fonds en comble tel qu'on le void, combien que ceux qui sont versez en l'art y remarquent tout plein d'erreurs tant par dedans que par dehors. A la vérité ces grands pièces méritent bien de passer par les mains de ceux qui ont fait leur apprentissage et coups d'essais en d'autres moindres suyvant le dire commun Italien 'gastando s'impara', qu'un tailleur avant que se randre bon maistre aura gasté assez de drap . . .'[14]

Unfortunately de Vigenère leaves us to guess the faults in this unconventional and thoroughly original building (Figs 59–63).

Serlio's proposals for a city palace for the King were rejected by 1546 when Lescot was appointed architect of the Louvre by François I (Figs 56–58). The scheme devised by Serlio in its massive scale took none of the topographical conditions of the western end of the city into account, and would have required drastic clearances in a populous quarter. The elevations of this forlorn project are the most developed and subtle of Serlio's blends of Italian and French building practice and architectural styles. The windows are of French proportions and the lofty pitched roof would have required the special carpentry techniques which Serlio met in France. The limited use of the orders to articulate key portions and give balance to the extensive elevation is a method of classicizing untried in

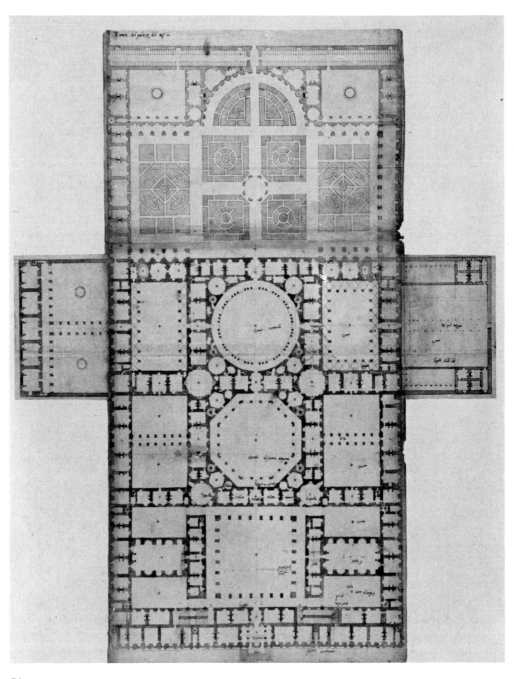

56
Sebastiano Serlio. Plan of a City palace for the King. (Avery ms. n° LXII)

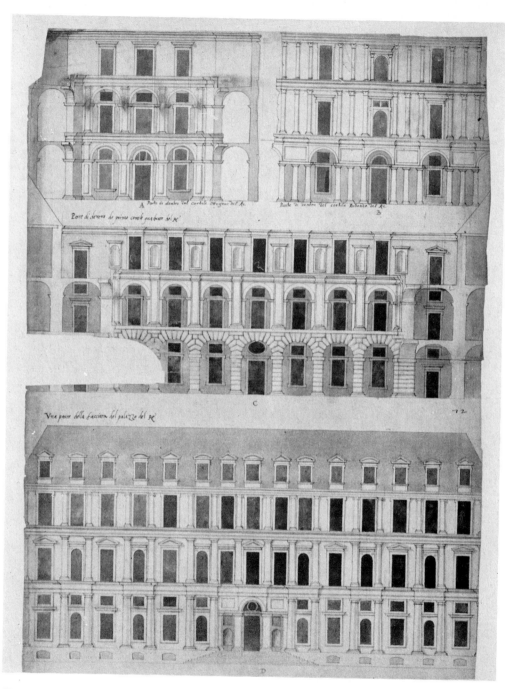

57
Sebastiano Serlio. Elevations for the City palace for the King. (Avery ms. n° LXXII)

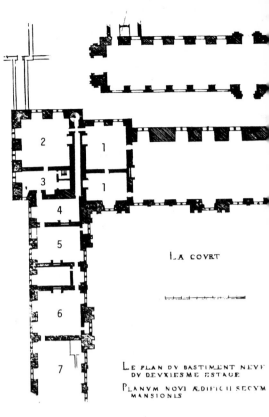

LA COVRT

LE PLAN DV BASTIMENT NEVF
DV DEVXIESME ESTAGE

PLANVM NOVI ÆDIFICII SECVM
MANSIONIS

58
Sebastiano Serlio. Section of an elevation of
the City palace project. (Avery ms.
n° LXXIIIa)

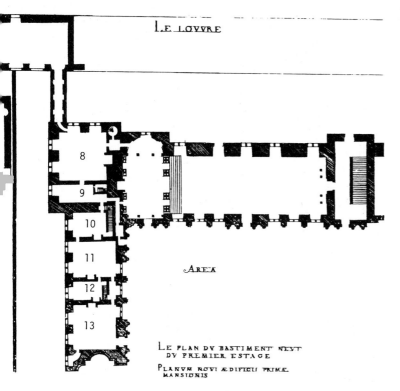

LE LOVVRE

8

9

10

11

12

13

AREA

LE PLAN DV BASTIMENT NEVF
DV PREMIER ESTAGE
PLANVM NOVI ÆDIFICII PRIMÆ
MANSIONIS

59
The Louvre. Plans of the
ground and first floors.
Engraving from *Le Premier
Volume des plus excellents
Bastiments de France* by
Androuet du Cerceau of
1576.

France where the previous and contemporary style was for continuous friezes with pilasters in each bay.[15] The literate proportions of the sparingly used orders gives Serlio's project its pseudo-Italian appearance, for the masses are unlike any Roman or Venetian palace. The wall section (Fig. 58) shows a further refinement by Serlio to give relief to his façade design, which is not apparent from his elevation drawing. By staggering the advance of each of the floors, Serlio showed the Court one way of further animating a monotonous wall, and this idea was pilfered by Pierre Lescot. Lescot was a personality whose qualities of mind were of more interest to François I, than an aged Italian architectural popularizer who did not express himself in French.

According to a Venetian ambassador, François I had the ability to discourse pertinently on all of the arts. The nickname of his nominee for the design of the Hôtel de Ville, the 'Boccador', is just one reference to the qualities of eloquence and erudition which we know could impress François I in a servant or courtier. Blaise de Vigenère's characterization of Lescot as a talented draughtsman, with perhaps a sound theoretical grasp of principles of architectural style, but with no practical or technical expertise, would help to explain the partnership of a royal favourite with broad artistic talents[16] with Jean Goujon. Jean Martin's translation of Vitruvius, published in 1547, has woodcut illustrations made by Goujon which required the sculptor's own reading and interpretation of the text. The hellenism of some of Goujon's bas-reliefs complements contemporary

60

The Louvre. Elevations of the west and south fronts with the *pavillon du roi*. Engraving from *Le Premier Volume des plus excellents Bastiments de France* by Androuet du Cerceau of 1576.

developments in theatre and literature at Court[17] and shows Goujon, if proof were needed, to have been both practician and connoisseur of ancient art, a distinguished junior partner to Lescot.

The chronology of the building of the Louvre under Lescot has been clearly established from archival sources, but one important document has been lost, the contract for a more limited house which Lescot presented to François I in the year before the King's death in 1547.[18] Henri II wanted the programme expanded and masonry contracts from 1551 and 1556 with agreements between Lescot and Goujon for the sculpture have survived.[19] The initial project of 1546 is thought to have been for a square courtyarded house, not much bigger and following the lines of the medieval Louvre and it was François I who ordered the demolition of the keep in the middle of the courtyard and of the west and south wings.[20] Only the west wing and the 'pavillon du roi' were built before Lescot's death in 1578, but the south wing was completed almost exactly according to Lescot's intentions by his assistant and successor in charge of the Louvre from 1582, the engraver du Cerceau's eldest son, Baptiste.

Jacques Androuet du Cerceau's engraving of the outer west and south fronts with the 'pavillon du roi' in the middle (Fig. 60) is the best record of these façades, which were austere in contrast to the densely ornamented courtyard elevations (Figs 63–65). Cost would have been one reason against cladding both sides of the Louvre with relief sculpture and pilasters,

84

FACIES GEOMETRICA ILLIVS
PARTIS PAVILIONIS QVÆ
FLVMEN RESPICIT

FACE GEOMETRALE DV
PAVILON DV COSTE DE
LA RIVIERE

61
The Louvre. South elevation of the *pavillon du roi*. Engraving from *Le Premier Volume des plus excellents Bastiments de France* of 1576.

85

62
The Louvre. West front about 1660. Engraving by Israel Sylvestre.

but there must have been a further scruple in Lescot's mind suggested by Serlio, who had written that the public face of a gentleman or lord's house should not be so rich or ostentatious as to provoke jealousy or contempt. Hierarchical notions or architectural decorum pervade Serlio's writings on architecture and, in simplistic terms, the architect was urged to devise a style appropriate to each commission, for the town or the country, for the class of the patron and the function of the structure. The repertoire of classical ornament, as enlarged for his northern European readers who had never seen Italy, made masons and amateur architects aware of new expressive possibilities in wall decoration; in our discussion of late sixteenth-century aristocratic *hôtels* we shall see the currency of ideas where the use of the most intricate and pretentious classical ornament was viewed as suitable only on the buildings of the most noble.

The outer face of Lescot's west wing, on the left of the Pavillon du Roi in du Cerceau's engraving (Fig. 60), was plainer than the south front executed later by Baptiste Androuet du Cerceau,[21] to make the grand angle with the Royal apartments the more imposing and prominent, and the contrast with the courtyard façade the more dramatic. The decoration of the Pavillon du Roi was calculated to be legible from the other side of the river, with bold rusticated quoins and broad blank friezes dividing the floors underlined by narrow classical cornices. The large chamber which crowned the structure was an imposing belvedere with clear views over the countryside of the Left Bank and west along the river to Chaillot. The use to which this chamber was put is not known and it may never have been decorated inside. As shown by Androuet du Cerceau (Fig. 61), the Pavillon du Roi

63
The Louvre.

might be thought to have looked top heavy. The Louvre garden was a small space between the Pavillon du Roi and the river, whose greatest width was the length of the Petite Galerie (Fig. 62). Goujon made a woodcut for Martin's edition of Vitruvius to illustrate Vitruvius' point that statues on the pediment of a temple on a narrow street should be taller than normal to be seen properly at the imposed acute angle. Seen near to and below from the garden by the King or the Court, the proportions of the crown of the Pavillon du Roi should have looked satisfactory.

Possible relationships of Lescot's Louvre with the styles of the Renaissance architecture in other countries have never provided an insight into Lescot's architectural background or thought. There are no respectable sources either for the composition as a whole, or evident quotations by Lescot in any of his combinations of decorative detail on the courtyard front (Fig. 63). A project as much *en vue* as the new Louvre at the time of its design and building was likely to be heterogeneous from a designer devising and refining his ideas on the drawing board, and with advice on points of iconographical and possibly architectural details being proffered by men at the artistic heart of the Court like Ronsard.[22]

The elevation is nine bays wide, and in height has a ground and first floor of equal height, with an attic of half the height of the two main floors. The court front has subtle overall relief with the ground floor and the three pedimented frontispieces slightly projecting from the alignment of the rest of the first floor and attic. These gradations were not over emphasized by Lescot, for with even or weak light or with direct sunlight on the façade, these volumes are indistinct. The main horizontals of the design are the friezes and cornices above the ground and first floors; the ground-floor frieze and cornice is broken in the central bay of the three frontispieces which creates a more distinctive vertical accent for these advances. The idea of the shallow ground-floor arcade might have come to Lescot from the less refined Hôtel de Ville, but the slight recessions in the first floor and attic must have been adapted by Lescot from Serlio's project.

The distinctive use of the orders on Lescot's Louvre has been the object of much comment because of his use of the two most decorative of the orders, the Corinthian for the ground floor and the Composite on the first floor. A ground floor of a contemporary Italian palace would have the Doric on the ground floor with the Ionic for the first floor, obediently following the vertical sequence of the orders set by the Colosseum and repeated by architectural writers of the fifteenth and sixteenth centuries.[23] Lescot knew the true classical prescription for the orders on a tall elevation, but ignored it for at least two reasons. Firstly, the Corinthian and Composite used together produced decorative consistency in the make up of their capitals, and secondly they were thought of as the most evolved of the classical orders. Single pilasters divide the bays, with paired columns used to give greater relief on the frontispieces, where on the ground floor are doorways; that on the right-hand side leads into the double ramp of the Henri II staircase (Figs 59 & 56) and the other two would be opened for grand ceremonial occasions held in the Salle des Caryatides on the ground floor (Figs 59, 67–68).[24] The result of the use of columns on the frontispiece is to give the entrance bays an appropriate architecture of two tiers of triumphal arches.

Pierre Lescot never devoted himself entirely to architecture, and the number of commissions he is known to have accepted is fewer than six,[25] but the greatest loss is his copiously illustrated architectural treatise which on his death was inherited by his nephews, and which contemporaries hoped would be published, but the manuscript has disappeared without trace.[26] His book should have shown his knowledge and practice of a broader range of styles than the elegant or 'delicate' manner which he developed for his partnership with Jean Goujon, and to accommodate and complement Goujon's relief sculpture. The only evidence of his range is the Château de Valléry, designed by Lescot for one of Henri II's favourites the Maréchal de Saint-André, which in form has many similarities to the Louvre, but there Lescot used a rusticated decorative idiom with few classical motifs, a style appropriate for the country seat of a military leader.[27]

The sources, style and iconography of the sculpture on and in the Lescot wing of the Louvre have been discussed at length by historians and art

64
The Louvre.

65
The Louvre.

historians.[28] The allegorical figurative reliefs on the courtyard façade have been described as 'a paean of praise to monarchical government, its pretensions, prerogatives and obligations as well as the blessings it assures'.[29] The achievements conveyed by the figures in the attic are *Abundance* in the south pediment personified by *Neptune* and *Ceres* underneath, *Victories* with the royal escutcheon fill the central pediment with *Mars* and *Bellona* flanked by captives underneath, and *Science* in the north pediment celebrates the intellectual prowess of the French personified by *Archimedes* and *Euclid* accompanied with a *Genius* reading and a *Genius* writing (Fig. 64). Most of the attic figures are loosely based on the *ignudi* in Michelangelo's Sistine Chapel ceiling. A number of minds may have contributed to devising the overall iconographical scheme and to the selection of attributes, but Lescot's role was primordial in all matters of the design.

The caryatid portico at the north end of the Salle des Caryatides on the ground floor is usually labelled as by Jean Goujon in general histories of art (Fig. 67). The agreement for these sculptures made on 5 September 1550 between Lescot and Goujon is enlightening on its design and purpose.[30] The Salle des Caryatides is described as 'la grande salle de bal', and the balcony of the portico was to be a minstrel's gallery for oboeists and other kinds of musician; the sculptor should have been competent to design a caryatid portico symbolic of victory, but the text specifies that Lescot had passed on a plaster model for Goujon to follow. Illustrated editions of Vitruvius usually showed their editor's idea of the appearance of the antique caryatid portico described by Vitruvius,[31] and Goujon's woodcuts for Martin's edition of 1547 arguably are the finest of all the sixteenth-century versions of the subject, but Lescot introduced significant modifications and corrections in his design passed to Goujon in 1550.[32] The Louvre's caryatid portico was the first time a passage from Vitruvius had been used to recreate an antique monument on the monumental scale and in a permanent form.

At the opposite end of the ball room from the caryatid portico was the 'Tribunal' (Fig. 68) and dais, with a curious architectural superstructure whose purpose is unknown, but which would have made an imposing setting for an entrance by the monarch from the state apartments behind, through one of the doors on either side of the fireplace in the middle. The architecture of this set piece was of two sets of groups of four fluted Doric columns on either side of a vaulted arch. A source for the composition which has been suggested is Giulio Romano's portico on the garden side of the Palazzo del Tè at Mantua,[33] but here the context is very different, and until the use of this ensemble is discovered, the iconography of this distinctive piece of architecture must be left to speculation.

The Louvre's main staircase, built from 1551 onwards behind the caryatid portico at the north end of the Lescot wing, cannot have been Henri II's Queen Catherine de Medici's favourite way of climbing to the

66
The Louvre. Vault of the Henri II staircase.

67(a)

67(b)
The Louvre. Caryatids portico. (a) Drawing by Androuet du Cerceau. (b) Present remodelled condition.

68
The Louvre. Tribunal. Drawing by Androuet du Cerceau.

first floor. The compartments of the vaults were filled with emblems of pleasure and the hunt, fauns, Pans and dogs, but worst from her point of view was the blatant celebration of the King's mistress with the goddess Diana (Fig. 66). The only other glories of the inside of Henri II's Louvre to survive are two wood coffered ceilings from the King's 'chambre de parade' and the 'antichambre du roi' from the Pavillon du Roi[34] (Figs 69–70). The carving of the former was by the Italian Scibec da Carpi, but once again a contract of 1556 shows the design was by Pierre Lescot.[35] The outside cornice of consoles and garlands, the pairs of square coffers close to the corners of the outer zone and the central rectangular frieze decorated with laurel leaves are quotations or derivations from antique architecture used in a new context. The delicately carved friezes of the coffers are more correctly Roman than anything seen in France before, even amongst Scibec da Carpi's previous work for the Crown at Fontainebleau, and has few equivalents in Italy. The largest of the suits of armour, shields and other trophies were separately carved, and the whole ceiling was assembled in such a way that it could be dismantled for cleaning.[36] In the reign of Charles X it was removed from its original location to the third chamber behind the colonnade of the east front. The ceiling of the 'chambre de parade' was entirely gilded, and one day its brilliance might be restored. That of the 'antichambre du roi' also has suffered and now has wholly

93

69
The Louvre. Ceiling of the
chambre de parade du roi.

unsuitable paintings by Georges Braque in lurid blue and white fitted in its panels. The carving was probably by Jean Goujon with Etienne Cramoy, and the design should be attributed to Pierre Lescot.

It is easier to describe the Louvre than to attempt an analysis of its style. The courtyard façade is the most sumptuous and dense display of columns and pilasters with figurative and architectural sculpture on any palace of the age, but it is not as richly festooned as Lescot intended for the blank frieze at the bottom of the first floor was to have carving.[37] Blaise de Vigenère had heard criticisms of Lescot's Louvre, and it is his characterization of

70
The Louvre. Ceiling of the *antichambre du roi*.

Lescot as a man more versed in drawing than the rules and techniques of classical architecture and of building, which points to Philibert de l'Orme as the anonymous objector.

De l'Orme was the architect of all the royal building projects under Henri II except the Louvre, where François I's choice of designer was respected by his son. The nine books of de l'Orme's *Architecture* published in 1567 is a remarkable compendium of practical building and stylistic advice based on his own experience and illustrating houses designed by himself. His text is full of calls to patrons to employ a man like himself, who had a first-hand knowledge of antiquity, of mathematics, and architectural theories, and above all with a sound knowledge of building materials and conditions in France, and for patrons not to be impressed by or employ 'faisseurs de desseins'.[38] The tenth chapter of his first book is a tirade against 'parrots' who may speak well and draw nicely, but whose presumption in calling themselves architects infuriated de l'Orme. Pierre Lescot was not the only courtier known to have taken a special interest in architecture; one of the Pléiade Etienne Jodelle, the poet and dramatist who introduced a pure form of Greek tragedy into the French theatre, listed architecture as one of his accomplishments and is associated with the design of one of the most ostentatious country houses near to Paris during the late 1550s.[39] In de l'Orme's mind, an overlay, richness or massing of ornament was a trait of the imposter who could not provide a rational basis for his design. He must have been contemptuous of Lescot before all others, but his book only describes his views on how things should be done and he avoids offending the Royal family by razing the Louvre with his thinking on architectural reason. De Vigenère refers to faults both on the inside and on the outside detected by 'ceux qui sont versez en l'art'. De l'Orme would have objected to the use of a caryatid portico as a minstrel's gallery in the ball room, for the one erected by the Greeks had been a public monument of triumph in the open air and set nobly on a podium. For Anet about 1548 de l'Orme designed a frontispiece for the centre of the main block, which might be seen as his corrective to Lescot's on the Louvre. De l'Orme opted for a correct sequence of columns one above the other, the Doric below, with Ionic and Corinthian above, and each given appropriate relative proportions, the Doric being the shortest and the Corinthian at the top the tallest. Crowning a frontispiece of columns with weaker half pilasters must have been viewed disfavourably by de l'Orme in Lescot's design. Other solecisms at the Louvre which can be sifted are so inconspicuous that Lescot ought not to be remembered as a gentleman or amateur architect, with such a label's connotations. In its originality, Lescot's Louvre is a work of architecture which perfectly reflects the aspirations of contemporary poets for a great national revival of literature inspired by but not beholden to the precedents of antiquity.

The death of Henri II in 1559, after a jousting accident, led to the temporary disgrace of Philibert de l'Orme, marks the effective end of

Pierre Lescot's interest and activity in architecture and placed the King's widow, Catherine de Medici, in power for the rest of her life, in a position to try to satisfy her extravagant tastes and considerable building ambitions. The reigns of her sons, François II, Charles IX and Henri III have been called aptly the Age of Catherine de Medici.

CHAPTER IV

Haut-Bourgeois and Aristocratic Building, 1540–1600

1   Class, classicism, nationalism and anti-classicism

Renaissance Architecture encompasses as many distinctive national and local styles, Vitruvian, non-Vitruvian and anti-Vitruvian developments as there are European languages and dialects. The 'classical language of architecture' in the sixteenth century never developed a common usage agreed and understood by amateurs, scholars and practising architects. The example of the relationship between the archaeological surveying and research by Palladio and his own architecture is one of many enigmas; it is significant that he published his villas in 1570 with short, bald descriptive notices and made no attempt to describe his personal intellectual and creative methods. International architectural movements based on the inspiration of Greece, Rome or personalities did not develop in the sixteenth century, which might be described as an age of national and regional classicisms, and the architectural literature of the time illustrates more discordances and diversities than influences between Italian and northern European styles and practices. Philibert de l'Orme's *Architecture* was written for a French not a European public. Serlio's undogmatic pattern books were the only international publishing success in the field of architecture to reach patrons, architects and master masons[1] and to offer designs and models of windows or arcades which need not impinge on regional building customs, but Paris and the Ile de France had their own Serlio in Androuet du Cerceau whose *Livres d'Architecture* of 1559 and 1582 showed town and country houses in various French idioms and shorn of clear references to Italian villas and palaces.[2] Serlio was deeply conscious of the contrast between building and architectural style in Italy and France and in a circumspect manner sought to draw closer the 'modo di Francia' to the Bramantesque tradition in domestic architecture seen in the manuscripts of his sixth book which was never published.

A description of the architecture of Renaissance Paris is not the story of a coherent stylistic development. Social conditions can be used to outline the evolution of plan-types, but social attitudes and traditions can be made to help in elucidating the diversity of styles across the second half of the century or even within some of its decades. Architectural writers gave plenty of stern advice on the choice of sites, the need for prudence in selecting an architect who could be counted as both cultured and technically competent, and prudent over the dangers of overspending, but several sixteenth- and early seventeenth-century French writers on economic, legal and political matters made pertinent critical comments on the taste for antique and modern foreign art in general and building as a vanity in particular. It cannot be surprising to see more than one community of ideas dealing with an art as public, exclusive and expansive as architecture, and which could excite admiration, envy or contempt.

The influential publisher and classical scholar Henri Estienne, when writing an extensive commentary on Herodotus in the early 1560s, was concerned about indiscriminate adulation for the antique and Italian in painting and sculpture,[3] and the economist and political philosopher Jean Bodin, in a tract on the causes of monetary inflation of 1568, drew his readers' attention to the problem of importing instead of manufacturing luxury goods long before Henri IV or Colbert made it an issue in national policy; he complained of aristocrats' pride and profligacy as builders and collectors and surprises us by singling out Pierre Lescot as a great native painter.[4] Amongst the many texts which might be quoted from the time of the traumas of the religious wars, the most interesting is that by the Parisian Bernard de Girard, seigneur du Haillan (c. 1535–1610), a royal secretary to Henri, duc d'Anjou the future Henri III, historiographer to Charles IX, who ended his days as genealogist to the Order of the Saint Esprit for Henri IV.[5] In a brochure written in 1574 and published in 1586 called the *Causes de l'extreme cherté qui est en France* he wrote

'Let us now turn to the buildings of present times, then to their furnishings. It was but thirty or forty years ago that this excessive and magnificent manner of building came to France. Formerly our fathers were content to build a good house, a pavilion or a round tower, a menagerie and other accommodation needed to house themselves and their family, without erecting the superb structures as today with large main blocks, pavilions, courts, back courtyards, service courtyards, galleries, halls, porticoes, flights of steps, balusters and other such things. Not the slightest care is taken with the geometrical proportion in the architecture of the outside, which in many buildings has upset the commodiousness of the interior; once one knew nothing of confecting so many friezes, cornices, frontispieces, podia, pedestals, capitals, architraves, stylobates, flutings, mouldings and columns and, in brief, one was not aware of all of these antique manners of architecture which mean spending a great deal of money and which, more often than not, make the interior ugly in order to embellish the exterior; one knew nothing of putting marble or porphyry on fireplaces nor around the doors of houses, nor of gilding the beams and joists.

Girard was the most virulent critic to single out the classical style for special criticism. Others were less assertive but had their doubts over the wisdom of adopting an imported fashion which had proved costly to many whom they deemed vain or over enthusiastic. The Italian 'bloodsuckers' at the court of Catherine de Medici were blamed by Huguenot writers for many of the nation's ills,[6] and conspicuous or ostentatious extravagance rather than the continual warfare was the cause they favoured for the ruin of eight out of ten French noble families. François de La Noue (1531–91) and his *Discours politiques et militaires*, written in 1580 and published in 1587, is the best known of these and was the most influential book abroad on the plight of France. It contains these observations on the pitfalls of building and architecture, after some similar comments on clothes and before others on furniture and food.

'Let us now come to the second article of our vain expenses, consisting of the immoderate affectations that sundry have for stately buildings. For although it has been so from the beginning, yet it was little compared to our own times, when we see the qualities and the number of buildings surpassing olden times. And especially our Nobility have exceeded in this, rather for vain glory than any necessity. I suppose it is not much more than sixty years ago that architecture was restored in France, where before men had lodged grossly. But since then the fair traits of this art have been revealed, many have endeavoured to put them into practice. If none but some of the great and the rich had employed the abundance of their crowns upon such works, that would not have been reprehensible, considering they were ornaments both for the towns and for the countryside. But following their example the lesser rich, even the poor, have wanted to set their hands to such work, and without thinking were obliged to take on much more than they foresaw: and that not without repentance. The lawyers and above all the treasurers have likewise increased the ardour of the lords for building. For they say: "How is this? These men that are not so well established as us build like Princes, and shall we sit still?" and so envious one of the other, a multitude of fine houses have been built, and often by the ruin of revenue, which has gone into other hands, because of this vehement passion which they have for putting one stone on top of another. How many are they that have started sumptuous edifices, which have been left unfinished?, having come to their senses half way through their folly. In every Province we see but too many examples. It may be that some when they see themselves so well clothed and spangled in gold, have said "This cage is too small for so beautiful a bird, it must have a more stately one". To this reasoning some flatterer may have replied "Sir, it is a shame that your neighbour, who is no better than yourself, should be better housed. But take heart, for he that begins boldly has already done half of the work, and the means will not elude the wise man." He, feeling himself scratched where it itched, forthwith conceived in his imagination a design, which he began with pleasure, continued with pain, and completed in sorrow. Often it comes about that he who has built himself a house fit for a lord with an income of twenty-five thousand livres, which his heir, finding himself with one of only seven or eight hundred, and being ashamed to lodge his poverty in such stateliness, has sold it to buy another, suited to his income. And he that would not sell has been driven "to feed upon small loaves" (as one says) and he feasts his friends, when they visit, with discourses on architecture. When Father Jean des Antomeures (who was one of the most worthy men of our times) entered these magnificent houses and châteaux, where he saw lean kitchens, he used to say "Oh, to what purpose are all these fine towers, galleries, chambers, halls and closets, with the cauldrons so cold, and the cellars so empty? By the Pope's worthy pantofle (for that was his customary oath) I would rather dwell under a small roof, and hear from my room the harmony of the spits, smell the savour of the roast, and see my cupboard glorying in flagons, pots and goblets, than to dwell in these great palaces, to take long walks, and to pick my teeth fasting in the Neapolitan fashion." I accept the opinion of those who advise that if they build, it is on the condition that they sell little or none of their goods, and he who does otherwise, I refer him to the censure of Father Jean des Antomeures. I am well aware that one of the most remarkable things which one notices in France are the fine buildings strewn across the country, which are not to be seen elsewhere. But if one also counts how many of such splendours have reduced men to beggary, one will say the the product indeed is costly.'[7]

Care has to be taken when evaluating such texts, to understand the political background and the motives of each of the authors. In general, writers on both sides of the religious divide wrote in a similar vein, lamenting the profligacy of the old nobility and despairing of the temptation to compete with the contemptible class of rich lawyers, merchants, tax gatherers and Italian bankers. Girard and de La Noue were saddened by the decline both of the wealth and of the influence and prestige of the French nobility and aristocracy, and nostalgically saw the reigns of Louis XII and of François I as a last flowering of the natural, traditional and just order of France. The issues which led to the eruption of the Fronde can be traced back to the reigns of Charles IX and of Henri III. In a society where regulations were drawn up, but rarely obeyed, reserving the wearing of certain luxury cloths for the most noble, appearances were made to matter in the maintenance of the decorum of rank of an unstable hierarchy. The anatomy of class and privilege described by Claude Loyseau in his *Cinq Livres du droit des offices, suivis du livre des seigneuries et de celui des Ordres* of 1610 helps in an understanding of many of the internecine rivalries of the late sixteenth century in an age of numerous unholy alliances. In his *Traité de l'économie politique* published in 1615, Montchrestien fumed, 'At present it is impossible to distinguish by appearances. The shop keeper is dressed like a

71–72

Houses on the rue Saint-Denis and on the rue Neuve Notre-Dame, as published in Lenoir's *Statistique Monumentale du Vieux Paris*, 1867. These are the only detailed records of examples of substantial sixteenth-century bourgeois houses with elaborate classical decoration. Bernard de Girard's complaint that '. . . the interior (is made) ugly, in order to embellish the exterior . . .' cannot be made to apply to these compositions. The interior arrangements were not adjusted to make the façades symmetrical. The influence of Lescot's window mouldings on the Louvre is seen on the house on the rue Saint-Denis, which encourages a dating of 1555–1565. The house on the rue Neuve Notre-Dame is very difficult to date, but may have been built during the first half of the 1560s at the earliest.

The principal ornamentation of both houses is the
use of richly carved friezes and varied pediments,
with no attempt made to articulate the façades with
orders. Both houses might have been older
structures embellished by proud, but as yet,
unidentified owners.

gentleman . . . Moreover, who cannot see how this conformity of ornament does not introduce a corruption into our ancient discipline?' Social decorum must be considered in a discussion of the architectures of the second half of the sixteenth century in Paris where the scale and style of a building could be influenced by concerns remote from the 'classical language of architecture'. Girard's and de La Noue's words should not be seen as satires on building practice, for the example of Paris in their times yields many examples of the unfinished houses and the frequent changes of ownership mentioned by them. In the 1580s, when their essays were published, houses for royal, aristocratic and haut-bourgeois patrons were being built in distinctive and contrasting styles, which visibly reflects attitudes common to political writers and an architect of the status and calibre of Philibert de l'Orme, who built his own house in a manner he deemed appropriate to his resources and class (Figs 92–94).

2 Haut-bourgeois and aristocratic town houses, 1540–1600

A comprehensive and satisfactory architectural history of Renaissance Paris may never be written for there is no consistency in the documentary and graphic records of the best of bourgeois and aristocratic building in the capital. For every block and district of the Marais, les Halles, the quartier Saint-Honoré or the Left Bank there is either a documentary shortage, or a lack of drawings or engravings, or both. Little more than a dozen private houses built between 1540 and 1600 can be adequately described from both plans and elevations, and singling out those of which adequate records happen to have survived for a stylistic study has many pitfalls, if only because such a study can have none of the neatness of a limited chronological and topographical account. The architectural wealth of lost Paris can be imagined by reading down the long lists of the palaces and houses of French and foreign princes, archbishops, ambassadors, Royal favourites and bankers given by Henri Sauval, the first methodical historian of the city writing in the 1650s.[8]

Pierre de Bourdeille, seigneur de Brantôme, the best-known chronicler of the lives, loves and deeds of the prominent figures at the French court in the sixteenth century, enthusiastically wrote of Fontainebleau having thirty houses or rather 'palaces, vying with each other to please their King, of Princes, Cardinals and great Lords'. In his notice on the château published in 1579, Androuet du Cerceau wrote of François I's feeling that at Fontainebleau he was *chez soy*, of how the best of his collections were bought for Fontainebleau and mentioned the many lords who built there because of the King's preference for the place. Du Cerceau added, 'But since the death of the late King François [in 1547] the place has not been so habituated nor frequented, which will be the reason for its decay with the passage of time, as at very many other places which I have seen, because they are no longer lived in.' This prophecy was fulfilled, for all of the great houses have disappeared, and the town and the precincts of the château now reveal almost nothing of its architectural eminence in the first sixty years of the sixteenth century. The most vivid record of these 'palaces' is a group of late seventeenth- and early eighteenth-century surveys which show the impressive size and plans of some of these 'palaces' (Fig. 73). They are of central importance in expanding the fragmentary story of aristocratic town-house planning during the reign of François I, when the social and diplomatic life of the court had not yet settled in Paris, which had happened by the time du Cerceau made his comments during the reign of Henri III 'the most Parisian of all French Kings'. In the earlier reign the need to be near the King and to be able to entertain him lavishly when he was *a l'aise* was the motive for most of the dignitaries who invested in building at Fontainebleau rather than Paris. The Chancellor Antoine Du Prat took over the Hôtel de Sens in the capital after the death of Tristan de Salazar, but with a substantial *hôtel* which he retained at Fontainebleau for himself, his secretariat and household, his role as François I's most trusted political and financial adviser was made more efficient and closer, a forerunner of the ministries built at the next surrogate capital of France – Versailles.[9] Little is known of the stylistic details of the houses built for princes, cardinals and royal mistresses on spacious sites close to the château,[10] except the opulent 'Grand Ferrare' or the urban château built between 1542 and 1546 for the Papal Nuncio, Cardinal Ippolito d'Este recorded by the luckless Serlio in the manuscripts of his sixth book.[11] (Fig. 75)

The form and arrangement of the Hôtel de Ferrare are of fundamental importance for the study of subsequent developments in the capital, where its layout might have been imitated more often had the *lotissement* plots been more spacious. The courtyard was almost square, with a *corps de logis* about 38 metres in length and lateral wings just under 30 metres long, the right-hand wing containing the offices. Only the *corps de logis* had cellars; the ground floor was raised five French feet above the level of the courtyard, and the single storey was 16 French feet in height to the ceiling. Built in sandstone with no classical refinements such as columns or pilasters the main block had restrained colour accents with red brick being used for the entablature mouldings and the dormer windows. The earliest known contract for the house from March 1542 states that the dormers were to be copied from those of the Hôtel of Ambroise Le Veneur, Cardinal of Lisieux which recently had been completed at Fontainebleau, an interesting early example of a component in a design being quoted from a building where the results were admired or considered satisfactory, and which saved the parties to the contract from the trouble of drawing up specifications. The same contract only describes the main block and the offices; the gallery wing with the centrally-planned chapel at its end, the first in French architecture, must have been a part of Serlio's contribution

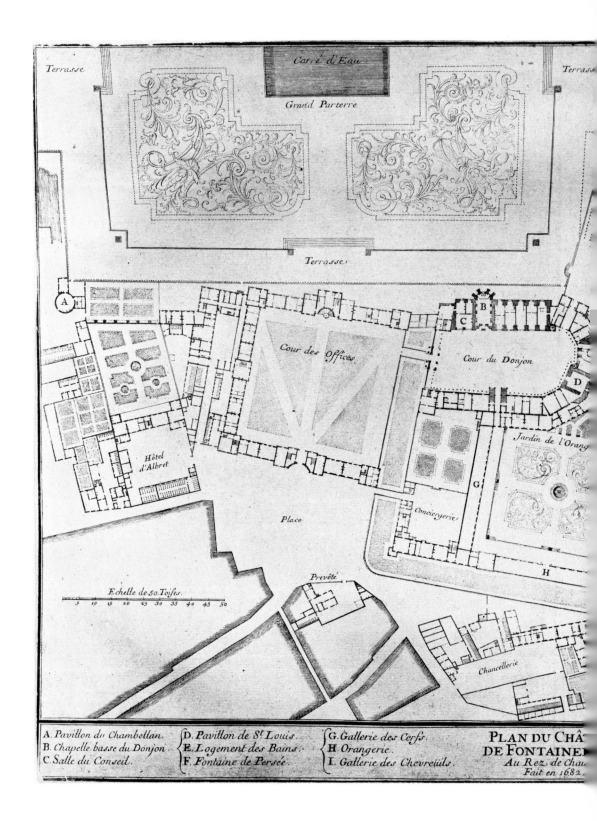

Terrasse

Carré d'Eau

Grand Parterre

Terrasse

Terrasse

A

Cour des Offices

Cour du Donjon

B
C

D

Jardin de l'Orang

Hôtel
d'Albret

G

Conciergerie

H

Place

Prevôté

Echelle de 50. Toises.

5   10   15   20   25   30   35   40   45   50

Chancellerie

A. Pavillon du Chambellan.
B. Chapelle basse du Donjon.
C. Salle du Conseil.

D. Pavillon de St. Louis.
E. Logement des Bains.
F. Fontaine de Persée.

G. Gallerie des Cerfs.
H. Orangerie.
I. Gallerie des Chevreüils.

PLAN DU CHÂ
DE FONTAINE
Au Rez. de Chau
Fait en 1682.

106

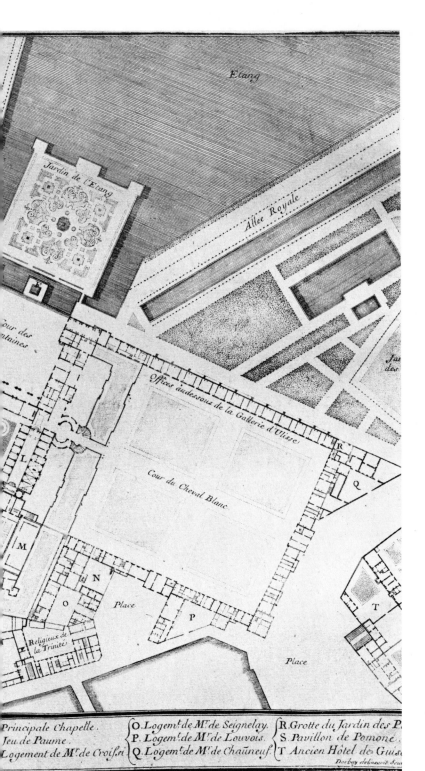

Etang

Jardin de l'Etang

Allée Royale

Cour des
Fontaines

Offices audessous de la Galerie d'Ulisse

Cour du Cheval Blanc.

R

Q

L

Jar
des

M

N

O

Place

P

T

Religieux de
la Trinité

Place

Principale Chapelle .
Jeu de Paume .
Logement de Mr de Croissi

O. Logemt de Mr de Seignelay.
P. Logemt de Mr de Louvois.
Q. Logemt de Mr de Chauneuf.

R. Grotte du Jardin des P.
S. Pavillon de Pomone .
T Ancien Hôtel de Guise

Dorbay delineavit Sculp

73
Fontainebleau. Plan of the
château and of houses in the
immediate vicinity.
Engraving by François
d'Orbay of 1682.

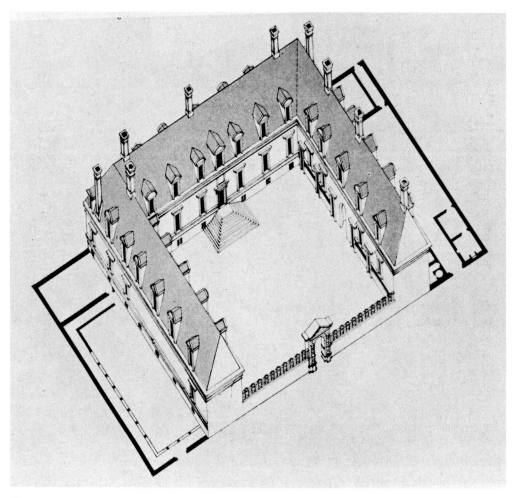

74
Hôtel de Ferrare, Fontainebleau. Bird's-eye view reconstruction from Rosci and Brizio.

to the design of the house for which he was paid by the Cardinal in April 1544. Another interesting feature in the planning of the 'Grand Ferrare' is the passage way through the middle of the office wing for carriages and carts into the stable courtyard behind, thus segregating all the services in the right-hand quarter of the site, with the kitchens the farthest removed from the Cardinal's apartments at the far end of the offices (Fig. 75). The *corps de logis* was an enfilade one room deep to give the best possible light, and with a garden front of just under 55 metres in length, it bisected the site leaving the garden completely private and free of the encumbrances seen in the plan of the Hôtel Le Gendre. The plan of the 'Grand Ferrare' is a distillation of many traditional elements and recent elements in French building, but was in many ways an ideal arrangement which could not be

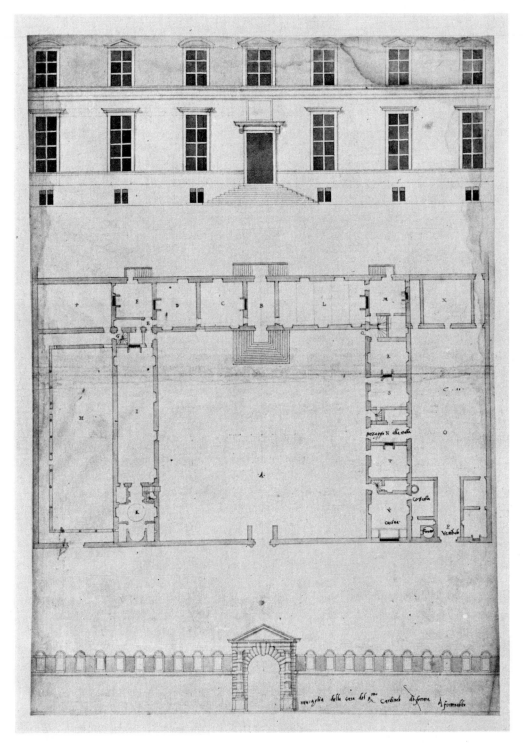

75
Hôtel de Ferrare, Fontainebleau. Courtyard elevation of *corps de logis* and plan by Sebastiano Serlio. (Avery ms. n° XI)

imitated widely; the house at Fontainebleau had a regular spacious site which meant that it could serve as a model for building in Paris only for the handful who had bought, or who accumulated after the first sales, more than one of the larger rectangular plots of the *lotissements*, so that there was enough space to separate services from the owner's living quarters.

Serlio made it his business to assimilate building practice in France and, despite its innovations, the French rather than 'imported' characteristics are more distinct in the plan and elevations of the Hôtel de Ferrare. The crenellated entrance screen has been seen before at the Hôtel de Cluny where there was little space and probably no wish to close the courtyard with a wing on its south side, but courtyard screens were common at farms, manors and country houses before and after the 1540s. The only surviving feature of the Hôtel de Ferrare is Serlio's boldly rusticated entrance arch exemplifying not only the temporal power and status of the owner, but also suggesting a country or rustic association (Fig. 76). The view of the 'Grand Ferrare' as a country house brought into the town is strengthened in its similarities with Saint-Maur-des-Fossés, the first of Philibert de l'Orme's major château commissions after his return from Italy, begun before 1541 for another Cardinal, Jean du Bellay, Bishop of Paris (Fig. 79). De l'Orme's first project for Saint-Maur was a rectangular courtyarded house and like the house at Fontainebleau it was to have a single main floor raised above ground level, on top of cellars. Charles IX in the 1560s referred to Saint-Maur as his *cassine*,[12] and antique and modern Italian ideas on the design and organization of a retreat or villa of a great man clearly were in de l'Orme's mind with the first project for Saint-Maur with its tall basement and clearly defined *piano nobile* distinguished by Corinthian columns and pilasters.[13] Ippolito d'Este would not allow Serlio to publish the Hôtel de Ferrare as it was built, because he felt its appearance might provoke scorn.[14] The Italian could well have been impressed by his brother Cardinal's house, with its like form and sophisticated demonstration of a correctly proportioned order on a fully extended and developed basement and superstructure, beside which the *corps de logis* of the Hôtel de Ferrare looked austere. The real splendours of the 'Grand Ferrare' were inside, as can be imagined from the description by Giulio Alvarotto, the Ferrarese ambassador, of the reception, given by Ippolito d'Este in honour of the King at the house in May 1546.[15] The project which must have given more satisfaction to Ippolito d'Este than his *hôtel* at Fontainebleau is the house and gardens of the Villa d'Este at Tivoli, famous within his own lifetime for the opulent decorations of its interiors and the sculpture, fountains and waterworks in the park as can be seen in Montaigne's account of his visit.[16] The Hôtel de Ferrare was completed shortly after the *lotissement* of the Culture Sainte-Catherine at a time when several of the class of lawyers and treasurers, singled out by De La Noue as the newly rich with building ambitions, were arranging for the design and construction of their new town houses in the capital, and prominent amongst them

76
Hôtel de Ferrare, Fontainebleau. Entrance gateway.

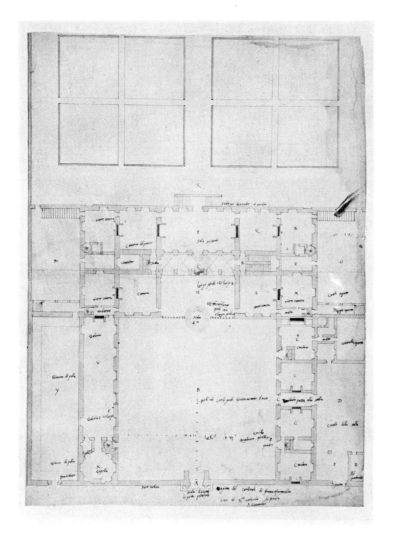

77
Hôtel de Ferrare,
Fontainebleau. Plan of an
enlarged project by
Sebastiano Serlio. (Avery
ms. n° XII)

was Jacques des Ligneris, President of the Parlement de Paris.

With five well-sited plots of the Culture Sainte-Catherine (numbers 27 to 31 in Fig. 18) des Ligneris and his unidentified architect had several options in planning and orientating the house, and they chose to make the entrance on the east side on a plan clearly adapted from the Hôtel de Ferrare (Figs 80–84). The Hôtel des Ligneris, later, and now the Hôtel de Carnavalet, is a reduced variant of the house at Fontainebleau with a courtyard of about 18 metres in width by 21 metres in length and a garden front of just under 30 metres. Like that 'Grand Ferrare' the main block faces an entrance screen, with a gallery wing on the left of the courtyard and a stable courtyard in the right-hand side of the site with a separate gateway to the street, and with the kitchens relegated to the basement in the south eastern corner. Crossing the court the main block was entered in the right hand

78
Hôtel de Ferrare, Fontainebleau. Elevation of a garden façade for the variant Fig. 77. Drawing of *c.* 1550. Private collection, London.

corner where there was the main staircase pavilion, an arrangement which avoided taking space from the suites of rooms of the ground and first floors. The main block of two equal floors, five bays wide, with a single-bay pavilion on the left for the spiral stair joining the gallery, and a two-bay pavilion on the right for the *escalier d'honneur,* must be the original form of des Ligneris' house, but the appearance of the main block above the first-floor cornice and of the gallery wing above the arcade are later alterations. The right-hand wing, which replaced the stable courtyard is the work of François Mansart of 1660–1661, and was further altered in a drastic restoration of 1866–1870. The balustrade above the first-floor cornice of the main block and the three pedimented dormers were added during the nineteenth-century restoration, and are copied from Jean Marot's engraved proposals of the 1650s for the remodelling of the house, which the nineteenth-century architects mistakenly believed to be a record of the original appearance of the Hôtel des Ligneris/Carnavalet before Mansart's additions. The late nineteenth century also saw the destruction of the series of decorative medallions, on the ground floor of the *corps de logis,* one of which is seen in Hénard's drawing (Fig. 81a). The enfilade of reception room, two further rooms and *cabinet* at the far end becomes a very familiar feature in the seventeenth century when the etiquette of how and where a lady or gentleman received their guests was fully evolved.[17] The main block of the Hôtel des Ligneris might be read from right to left as public to private rooms following the system which had evolved in the royal apartments in the Louvre.[18] The purpose or function of the gallery remains to be explained; the evolution of the gallery in the Middle Ages

79
Saint-Maur. Courtyard elevation of the *corps de logis*. Drawing for *Le Second Volume des plus excellents Bastiments de France* by Androuet du Cerceau of 1579.

and the Renaissance is a favourite matter of argument amongst architectural historians.[19]

The des Ligneris family retained seven servants for their needs and comforts, a number which may seem small when compared with aristocratic households of the period. An early eighteenth-century writer estimated that a third of the population of the city was employed in domestic service, and this might have been the situation in the mid-sixteenth century.[20] Des Ligneris was probably amongst those who arranged a *marché de pourvoierie* or a contract with an outside, professional buyer for the supply of fresh foods from the various Paris markets.[21]

The architecture of the entrance front and courtyard elevations were much altered in the seventeenth and nineteenth centuries. The rusticated entrance arch is datable to about 1550 and conventionally is attributed to Pierre Lescot, (Fig. 83) and there can be little doubt that a composition of rustication without an order must be the work of a court architect.[22] The publication of the 'rustic' and the 'delicate' doorways and arches in Serlio's *Livre Extraordinaire* at Lyons in 1550 made widely known the freedom and whimsy possible with the use of rustication. For the Hôtel des Ligneris the architect devised one of the most 'delicate' of 'rustic' designs in comparison with the massiveness and rougher finish of Serlio's models. The fine proportions and the eccentric cornice with its obtuse angle in the centre to suggest a pediment influenced the design of many gateways and arches built in Paris in the later sixteenth and seventeenth centuries.[23] The very

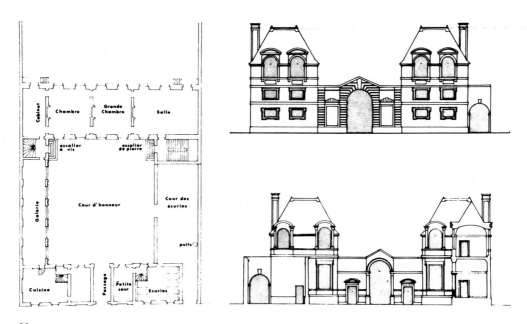

80

Hôtel des Ligneris (Carnavalet). Reconstruction drawing of its state in 1558, from the inventory of the possessions of Jacques des Ligneris. Jean-Pierre Babelon, inv., Jean Blécon, del.

satisfactory reconstruction of the entrance front, devised by Jean-Pierre Babelon and drawn by Jean Blécon (Fig. 80), shows an architecture of distinctive parts, with the immodest triumphal arch flanked by two pavilions made up of three storeys. Above the ground-floor storey is a mezzanine, which with the stables in the right-hand pavilion could not have expressed a floor level, and with another storey on top whose walls were the same height as the ground floor but aggrandized by pitched roofs and pairs of tall dormers with arched windows capped by shallow curved pediments. The top floor of the left-hand or south-eastern pavilion might have had a room used by des Ligneris' family or their servants, but the use of its twin over the north-eastern pavilion is puzzling since it has no covered access from the main block or from the other pavilion. It is unlikely that the north-eastern pavilion was built simply to complete the symmetry of the entrance front. The plan (Fig. 80) showing the extent of the development of the house is based on the inventory of the contents of the house made in 1558 after Jacques des Ligneris's death, and it may show the full extent of the first owner's intentions, but it must have been foreseen that the gallery wing would have to be balanced at least by an arcaded screen on the right-hand side of the courtyard.

The step-by-step approach to building a large Parisian *hôtel* is perfectly illustrated in the first hundred years of this house's history, with separate masonry contracts for each of the major elements of the plan being agreed at different times, usually within months or a few years of each other, but often the process took much longer and involved several owners using new architects. Only the main block was the subject of the 1548 contract,[24] and it was the fourth owner, Claude Boislève, who displaced the stable yard and had the courtyard completed and a pavilion built over the arch of a remodelled entrance front by François Mansart, work which was finished in 1661.[25] The story of French Renaissance architecture is full of unfinished grand designs and noble fragments of town and country houses begun 'with pleasure, continued with pain and completed in sorrow', but des Ligneris was one of the class whose buildings were built within their means and, according to De La Noue, tempted the nobility to their financial ruin.

The courtyard has its architectural variety, and it is known that there was another style employed for the original garden front of the *corps de logis* which was much admired, but inadequately described by Sauval.[26] It was of *crépi* or rough cast durable stone whose surface texture was certainly intended to create a 'rustic' effect, and our ignorance of its appearance is most regrettable. On a gateway, in Serlio's view, rustication created the impression of solidity or impregnability, and in this spirit it was used by Michele Sanmicheli in his famous city gates of Verona,[27] and by des Ligneris's architect on the entrance front. The façade seen by Sauval might have had rustication on the basement only, or extended up over the ground floor, or over all the floors, and if any of the windows and doors were framed by rusticated columns or pilasters with or without pediments, the back of des Ligneris's house would have been the first façade of the kind seen in France. Encasing classical façades in rustication became a 'leitmotif' for architectural popularizers such as Jacques Androuet du Cerceau later in the century.[28]

Successive owners made the Hôtel des Ligneris/Carnavalet the richest in sculpture of all sixteenth- and seventeenth-century Parisian private houses with reliefs on all four sides of the courtyard and on the outside. In France life-size figure sculpture was a feature of tombs, family chapels, church portals and some town halls, but des Ligneris's *corps de logis* is the earliest example of a private house with prominent allegorical reliefs, of Spring, Summer as Ceres, Autumn as Bacchus, and Winter (Fig. 81b). The fenestration of the *corps de logis* was designed like that of the Louvre to allow for sculpture, with panels of the same width as the windows, excluding their mouldings. The mason provided a perceptible extra thickness of stone in building the panels between the first-floor windows, and the reliefs were undoubtedly carved *in situ* by a sculptor using drawings by or imitating the style of Jean Goujon, and the intricacies of the drilling of Ceres' robes suggests a contribution by Goujon himself. In the spandrels of the courtyard side of the entrance arch are two exquisite reclining figures of *Fame* and on the long, narrow, trapezoidal keystone, which breaks the moulding of the arch, is *Authority* standing on a globe and holding a bow and mace, all appropriate symbols for des Ligneris the 'parlementaire' and ambassador to the Council of Trent.[29] The tympanum

81(a)

81(b)
Hôtel des Ligneris (Carnavalet). Elevations of the courtyard front of the *corps de logis*. (a) in 1847,
(b) present state.

82
Hôtel des Ligneris (Carnavalet). Elevation of the gallery by Jean Marot, (1655/1657.)

sculpture and the lions (which originally were on the court side of the entrance screen) were added by the Carnavalet (Fig. 83) in the late 1560s, and the crude and tedious cycle of Elements and Virtues by Gérard Van Obstal on the left and right wings of the courtyard, entrance front and on the south side of the south-eastern pavilion were part of the works of Claude Boislève executed in the 1660s.[30]

The considerable losses of mid and late sixteenth-century Parisian town houses inhibits most generalizations on the contemporary influence of any one house whose appearance is known or which happens to have survived, invariably in a much altered condition. However, there are several reasons for believing that des Ligneris' house was much *en vue* during and after its first phase of building. His next-door neighbour to the north, Guillaume Barthélemy, 'contrôlleur de l'ordinaire des guerres', was building a house of equivalent quality in dressed stone, decorated with pilasters[31] (plots 47 and 32 in Fig. 18). The building contract of 6 March 1547 for the Hôtel Barthélemy specifies that the boundary wall on the right of the main part of the house was to be 'of the same thickness as the building which monsieur the président des Ligneris has begun'. The introvert nature of Parisian building is seen when reading the contracts for the Hôtel Barthélemy, especially in the paragraph giving the specifications for the *corps de logis* where the master mason is directed to imitate work at two recently completed houses in the capital which were known to the patron.[32] A most curious detail to be gleaned from these contracts is the mention that some

83
Hôtel des Ligneris (Carnavalet). Entrance gateway from the street. Present condition.

of the window frames were to be covered in paper, rather than filled with glass.[33]

On plots 20 to 22 of the *lotissement* of the Culture Sainte-Catherine (Fig. 18) in 1546 Jacques Le Jay, a notary and royal secretary, and in 1551 Pierre Le Jay, a royal councillor and Guillaume Barthélemy's senior as 'trésorier extraordinaire des guerres', agreed contracts for the building of one of the largest houses erected in the area.[34] The general organization of Le Jay's buildings was the same as des Ligneris' house, with a large *corps de logis* bisecting the site with no classical ornament, a gallery on the left hand side of the court with an open arcade with pilasters at ground-floor level, and kitchens relegated to the end of the gallery with a service door to the rue des Francs-Bourgeois.[35] The Hôtel Le Jay must have been designed by a man abreast of developments at Fontainebleau, for two months after the original contract of July 1546 its terms were altered to specify that the ground-floor windows of the *corps de logis* were to have dressed stone sills, those of the first floor were to have mouldings in plaster and the dormers were to be in brick, a colour accent which is reminiscent of the Hôtel de Ferrare.[36] The imposing house built by the Le Jays is not one of the invisible houses of Renaissance Paris which has to be imagined in the

84
Hôtel des Ligneris
(Carnavalet). Cellars under
the *corps de logis*.
Nineteenth-century
engraving.

85
Hôtel Le Jay (d'Albret).
View of the roof and first
floor from the south.
Present condition.

mind's eye from information in building contracts. It survives in the most decrepit condition with the garden filled with industrial buildings (Fig. 85). The details given in the original building contracts will be an important source of reference for the architect when the Hôtel Le Jay is restored.

More vivid for setting the Hôtel des Ligneris in an architectural context is the small courtyard of a house on the rue Beautrellis, which was a part of the *lotissement* of the Hôtel Saint-Pol, a house most probably built in the second half of the 1550s or the 1560s (Fig. 86). All four sides of the court are decorated with arcades of plain twin pilasters and finely detailed capitals, an unmistakable quotation from the ground floor of des Ligneris' gallery. Open or closed ground-floor arcades of pillars or columns were common features of the ancillary wings of town and country houses by the time of the last years of the reign of François I and the reign of Henri II, but it is the consistent and persistent use of pilasters at the Hôtel des Ligneris, the invisible Hôtel Barthélemy, the Hôtel Le Jay and the house on the rue Beautrellis, on the courtyard elevations of de l'Orme's Saint-Maur or Lescot's Louvre which should intrigue architectural historians, for in no other country at that time do architects appear to have been so preoccupied with using the bastard form of column. Some practical reasons for this phenomenon will be suggested below, but it is remarkable that no sixteenth- or early seventeenth-century French writer on architecture seriously concerned himself with the use or abuse of the pilaster form, and

86
Courtyard arcades of a house n° 10 rue Beautrellis.

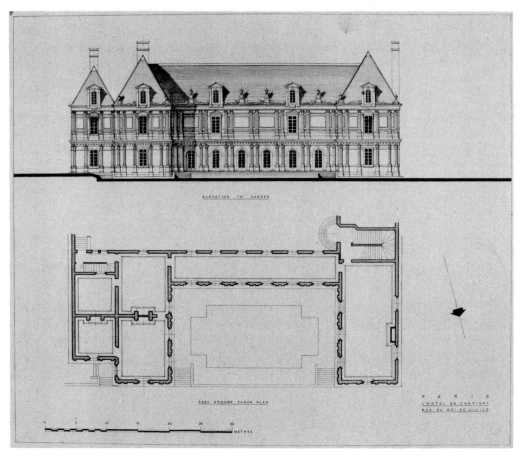

87
Hôtel du Cardinal de Meudon (de Birague, and later Chavigny). Elevation of garden front and plan.
Reconstruction drawing by A. Don Johnson.

instead of taking into account a prominent characteristic of the architectural styles of their time they chose to labour over the intricacies of the proportions of the orders of columns.

On the largest site of the Culture Sainte-Catherine (inscribed 'Hôtel du Roi de Sicile' in Fig. 18) the uncle of the Duchesse d'Etampes, Antoine Sanguin, Cardinal de Meudon built a house during the early to mid 1550s shown in a reconstruction drawing (Fig. 87). Sanguin was one of the few from a long established Parisian family to build a prestigious new town house in the sixteenth century,[37] and the considerable rise in his fortunes was due in great part to preferment at Court through his niece, whose house on the Quai des Augustins had many stylistic similarities to Sanguin's (Fig. 49). Like the Hôtel d'Etampes, the Hôtel du Cardinal de Meudon was two storeys in height with an elaborate architecture of pilasters, and it is a pity that a comparison of their stylistic details cannot be taken far because of the summary impression given in Sylvestre's engraving. The unknown architect of the Hôtel du Cardinal de Meudon was less gifted than Lescot in the design of arcades and the articulation of a façade with pilasters. The garden front of Sanguin's house owes more to the courtyard elevations of Ancy-le-Franc of the 1540s, which would have been known in Paris because of Serlio's contribution to the design, than to the elegance of Lescot's design of the Louvre. The system on the first floor, of window bays alternating with blank *tableaux* or panels separated by twin pilasters, is one which becomes familiar with the first of François I's châteaux in the Loire Valley at Blois and Chambord. If the participation of a Court architect in the design of the Hôtel des Ligneris is strongly suspected, Sanguin's architect was either not in touch or not in sympathy with the architectural thought and styles being discussed in aristocratic artistic circles of the early 1550s.

The plan of this house is unusual, but it is quite legible with its twin galleries on the ground and first floors connecting the west and east pavilions, the public and the private parts of the house. The option of a central staircase was open to the architect planning a building on a site as spacious as Sanguin's, but the main staircase was placed on the left-hand corner of the entrance court. This western pavilion, on the right-hand side of the drawing, had reception or public rooms on both floors, and the private apartments were at the opposite end of the galleries, with their own entrance from the court and a smaller staircase. The use to which the galleries were put remains conjectural. They were narrow and as far as we know without fireplaces, and they might have been intended as nothing more than richly-decorated corridors, for it is difficult to imagine banquets or dancing taking place in a space only four metres wide. Sanguin died in 1559 and is supposed to have left the house unfinished, but the Chancellor René de Birague who bought the property in about 1573 is known to have entertained Henri III in a gallery where he set up a magnificent display of plate of over a thousand pieces, most of which was broken by servants. That gallery might have been in the main block or in the one which Birague had built in the garden which is wider.[38]

A description of the styles of *haut-bourgeois* and aristocratic buildings of the second half of the sixteenth century in Paris is almost wholly centred on the small area of the Culture Sainte-Catherine. This part of the Marais in its first phase of development in the late 1540s and 1550s attracted the class spoken of by De La Noue and Dallington, and during the late 1550s, 1560s and 1570s there was a small but significant immigration into the area of nobility and aristocracy who bought and enlarged *hôtels* begun by the 'Lawyers and officers of the King's Money'. The Carnavalet bought des Ligneris' house and the Montmorency bought the Hôtel Le Jay and the Hôtel Barthélemy.[39] Some aristocratic building took place on the Left Bank during the troubled 1560s and 1570s,[40] but it was close to the Louvre in the 'quartier Saint-Honoré' and in the parish of Saint-Germain

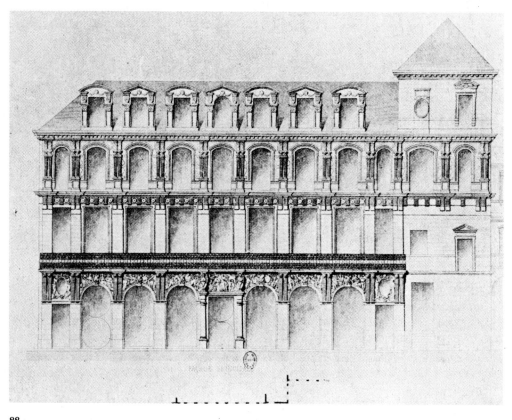

88
Hôtel du Faur. Elevation of north-facing gallery wing on the courtyard. Engraving from Albert Lenoir's
Statistique Monumentale du Vieux Paris of 1867.

L'Auxerrois that, as the notarial documents show, there was the greatest amount of building activity by leading personalities at the Court of Henri III during the 1580s. The architecture of just one of these houses is known (Figs 117–120).[41]

For the 1560s the solitary aristocratic *hôtel* which can be illustrated is the Hôtel du Faur (Figs 88–90) which is unlike any other known Parisian private house of the sixteenth or seventeenth centuries, and has been described as Toulousian rather than Parisian in style.[42] The patron, Jacques du Faur, was of an old and senior Toulouse family, 'la première maison de Robbe Longue en France', a leading jurist, member of the *conseil privé* of Charles IX from 1565 and the most trusted colleague and adviser to the Chancellor de l'Hôpital. The ground-floor arcade, now at the Ecole des Beaux Arts, is inscribed with the date 1567. On the eastern edge of the city on the Left Bank on the rue des Bernardins, du Faur built his unusual house in a quarter not associated with aristocratic building during the period.

89
Hôtel du Faur. Detail of gallery elevation from Lenoir.

90
Hôtel du Faur. Ground-floor arcade, now at the Ecole des Beaux Arts.

The elevation of the wing, recorded for Lenoir's *Statistique Monumental de Paris* before the destruction of the house in 1830, is a strange stylistic hybrid with different and contrasting decorative systems used for each of the four floors. Inspired by Goujon's work on the Louvre the ground-floor arcade has spandrel reliefs of *Victories,* allegorical figures of *Fame, Captives* and *Peace* reigning over the central doorway. It was the screen of a *cryptoporticus* in which Niccolo dell'Abbate painted an elaborate fresco cycle of pastoral mythological allegories. Dell'Abbate was the leading Italian painter in Paris, working for only the very great and powerful of the Kingdom, for the Constable Anne de Montmorency in the gallery of his largest Parisian house and in the chapel and duchess's room at the Hôtel de Guise.[43] In its sculptural and painted decoration the Hôtel du Faur was at the heart of Court art of the late 1560s, with patriotic and pastoral symbolism wholly in keeping with the literary tastes developed by Court poets. A member of the du Faur family, Guy du Faur de Pibrac, who was one of the most famous writers of pastoral verse in late sixteenth-century France, stayed in the house in 1576, and he may well have been the iconographer or inspiration of the sculpture and painting.[44] More than one literary figure is known to have taken an active role in devising costly sculptural programmes for the houses of proud but not always rich aristocrats.[45]

The wing of the Hôtel du Faur published by Lenoir ran from east to west facing north and at right angles to the street, and resembles in neither form nor detail the evolving 'classic' town house such as the Hôtels des Ligneris/Carnavalet or Le Jay. The Hôtel du Faur, on the edge of Paris, might have been conceived as a suburban or semi-rural retreat away from the populous parts of the city, as is suggested by its pastoral imagery in the *cryptoporticus,* where an eccentric and individual architecture could have

91
Hôtel d'Assézat at Toulouse. View of the courtyard.

been part of both its charm and sophistication to the eyes of contemporaries. The variety in the treatment of each floor is puzzling since Lescot had shown a way of coherently articulating or unifying in the vertical a richly decorated façade with the use of pilasters. At Toulouse the leading local architect Nicolas Bachelier concocted a unifying system of incorrectly proportioned Doric, Ionic and Corinthian applied columns for the three-storey courtyard elevations of the monumental Hôtel d'Assézat built between 1552 and 1562 where the influence of both Serlio and of Lescot's Louvre is clear in the combinations of shallow arcades and twin columns (Fig. 91).

As the engraving of the Hôtel du Faur's elevation looks so little like that of any other known Parisian sixteenth-century private house in form or detail it is tempting to ascribe its design to an architect from the south-west, where a variety of classical architectural styles were developed by men of letters and master masons which sometimes were more distinctly Italianate, with columns and loggias of arcades, than anything seen in the capital. The idea has to be questioned, for the 1560s was remarkable for flamboyant, classical, but hardly Italianate, architectural design by architects and architectural popularizers associated with the Court. De l'Orme's design of the Tuileries (Figs 124–125) was revolutionary in style with every conventional architectural member and small decorative feature remodelled, revised and combined in new ways. Androuet du Cerceau's albums of drawings of 'bastiments à plaisir' datable to the reign of Charles IX (1560–1576) are rich in fanciful designs, and is evidence of a short-lived fashion for bizarre combinations of exotic sculpture, oddly-proportioned orders and rich decorative textures on friezes and consoles, with rough and smooth rustication. The precise architectural context of the Hôtel du Faur remains to be defined, and the identification of its architect would be a great step forward. Closely-spaced windows on the first floor might have been chosen because the wing faced north and had no south front, to harmonize with the width of the *cryptoporticus* arcade, which obviated the need for a vertical order with a finely-observed Doric frieze being the only classical feature. The decorative system of the second floor can be described but cannot be interpreted. The meaning of the twin herms on fluted podia flanked by bows is obscure, but it is not likely to have been a decorative motif used at random; the mouldings of the windows on this floor, with their lugs and curved architraves, are quoted from Lescot's Louvre. The dormer windows were flanked by herms with stocky trapezoidal podia capped by triglyphs supporting broken alternating triangular and shallow curved pediments. By the 1560s it had become common practice to give the same height to the ground and first floors, but the proportions of the second floor and the dormer storey were not legibly related by a simple ratio to the heights of the floors below. The Hôtel du Faur is the most perplexing building in the history of sixteenth-century Parisian architecture.

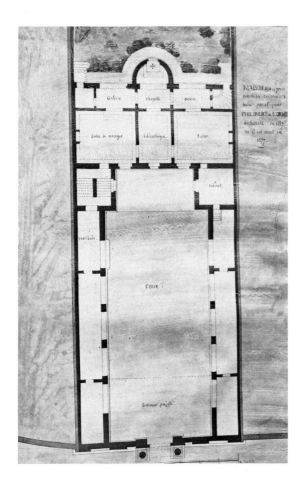

92
House of Philibert de
l'Orme on the rue de la
Cerisaie. Plan by
Vaudoyer.

The best documented scene of *haut-bourgeois* and aristocratic building in the late sixteenth century is still on the regular rectangular plots of the *lotissements* in the east of the city on the Right Bank, and they provide a convenient framework for descriptions and analyses of similarities and variety in planning and styles of elevations. In his *Architecture* of 1567 in stark contrast to his expert discourses on the technicalities of building, the fine points of the orders and his accounts of his most prestigious country house commissions, Philibert de l'Orme published woodcuts illustrating the house which he had designed and had built for himself about ten years earlier (Figs 92–94) on one of six long but narrow sites (about 16 metres) on the north side of the rue de la Cerisaie, a part of the *lotissement* of the Hôtel Saint-Pol (Fig. 17). The plan of the house, with *corps de logis* set back from the street between a forecourt and a garden at the back, is now familiar, but its austere appearance might be thought surprising from a man of de l'Orme's wealth and architectural culture, but as always he had good, clear, practical reasons to recommend his composition to his readers. De l'Orme is the best guide to the house and its architecture.

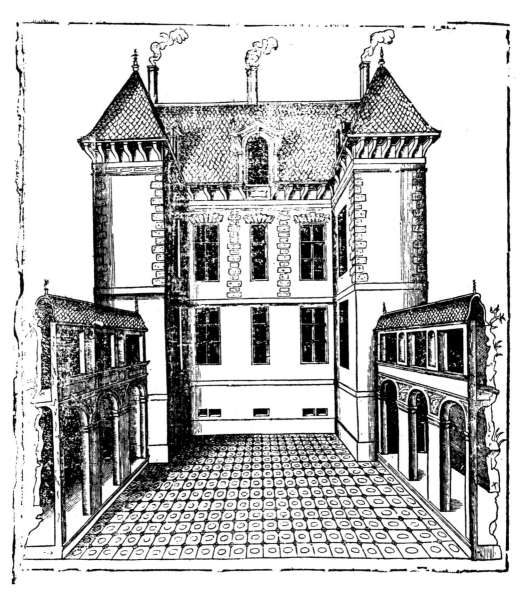

93
House of Philibert de l'Orme. View of the courtyard from his *Architecture* of 1567.

'Some might be thinking, after having read what I have written on the façades of buildings, to show the arrangements of windows, that I want to oblige them, or even compel them, to put columns and pillars on the façades of houses, which I have not claimed at all: for all those who wish to spend modestly have no need of such refinements and enrichments on the façade of a house, just as their resources are unable to meet such great expenditures: but it is quite true that the composition and order of windows, which will be set in the façades of houses, ought to conform

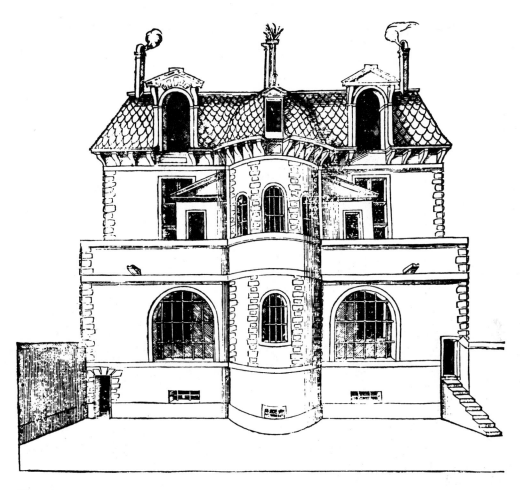

94
House of Philibert de l'Orme. Elevation of the garden front from his *Architecture* of 1567.

to such proportions and measurements, so that which one sees on one side might be seen on the other without columns or pillars, which is the manner sought, and it can be seen clearly in the next illustration (Fig. 93): in it I put, on the first floor, windows with mullions and transoms only: and on the second I show you how you might have designed between these windows, courses of stone, without the forms of pillars, capitals and other such things: and further windows are set into the roof and, should you wish, can be in dressed stone, in the rustic manner, or even quite plain, as the corners of the building can be treated. You see as well at the entablature of the whole building, on which rest the joists and the dormers, in case anyone should put cornices there, I have put mutules there in the form of scrolls to decorate and to make the house more attractive. I offer you also in this illustration square pillars connected by arches to create a peristyle below and a gallery above, all without columns, nor pedestals, capitals and cornices: this is to show how the learned and expert architect can devise an elegant building, without great expense, that will look as good as others which are much more elaborate: so you can see and judge in the next illustration.

'Since I am dealing with this purpose, I will finish by showing you the other side of the house, which faces the garden (Fig. 94). In the middle of it I have put a round tower, whose first (ground) floor serves as a chapel with a gallery in front of it with openings and windows of a different kind from the others: for they are curved, and do not have a height greater than their width: I have given them such great width to make the gallery more pleasant: nevertheless it is graceful and of great beauty just as it is: but it is much more so when the original is seen, than can be gleaned from the representation of it which you will see following. On the second floor of the tower is a very solid closet, being vaulted in dressed stone below and above, and well secured. On either side are other closets and terraces: and behind are the main living quarters of the house: all of it being, whether windows, entablatures or dormers, done (as you see in the illustration) in thoroughly good materials with great competence, as much in the cellars as in other places. You should know that all this is as it has been done for myself, being my own home, as you see it in the preceding and following illustrations.'

Philibert de l'Orme was too summary in justifying why his simpler classical and unclassical forms are to be seen as beautiful, but his insistence that good architecture can be achieved within strict financial limitations is a result of his experience in designing and organizing large' and small building programmes. At Anet, for Diane de Poitiers, Philibert did not launch the building of the whole scheme at the beginning, but made sure that the *corps de logis* was complete before passing contracts for the less essential entrance pavilion.[46] His business-like approach shows a clear sense of priorities in proceeding with building, and many apart from des Ligneris followed his advice before the publication of his book, and probably consulted him. In the text accompanying the woodcut showing the wing which he had hoped to build to close the courtyard of his own house, on the rue de la Cerisaie (Fig. 96), he mentioned his activity as a designer of middle-class houses, all of which have disappeared, but which can be read of in documents.[47]

In unambiguous terms de l'Orme told his readers that intelligent planning and good building could produce architecture to be admired, without any need for elaborate classical trappings. The house built about 1576 for Médéric de Donon, sieur de Châtres en Brie and of Loribeau, a Royal Councillor and Controller General of the King's buildings, on plots 57 and 50 of the Culture Sainte-Catherine, is a perfect example of the influence of de l'Orme after his death in 1570[48] (Figs 97–99). The site is

95
House at 20 rue Ferdinand Duval in which Philibert de l'Orme was staying in 1546. (Compare with the design of the garden front of his own house.)

96
House of Philibert de l'Orme. Unexecuted street front on the rue de la Cerisaie, from his *Architecture* of 1567.

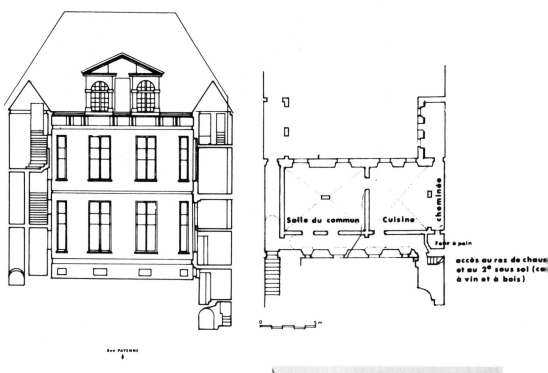

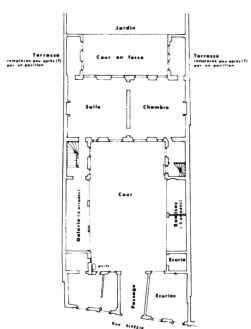

99
Hôtel de Donon.
Courtyard front of the *corps
de logis*.

97
Hôtel de Donon. Courtyard front of the *corps de logis* and plans. Reconstruction drawing. Jean-Pierre Babelon, inv., Jean Blécon, del.

134

98
Hôtel de Donon. View of the roof of the *corps de logis* on the garden side.

only slightly wider than was de l'Orme's, the *corps de logis* is in the form of a pavilion built well back from the street, but leaving room for a private garden in the western half. The site for Donon's house was much less spacious than the neighbouring Hôtel des Ligneris/Carnavalet, but the Hôtel de Donon was planned and organized with few differences. In the basement of the main block were the kitchens and a servant's hall, much closer to the reception rooms and private apartments than at the more prestigious Hôtels des Ligneris/Carnavalet or Le Jay. Otherwise the 'classic' formula of the plan of des Ligneris's house is repeated, with the stables to the right of the entrance, a gallery on the left and staircases in the left- and right-hand corners of the courtyard. The main block has clear rhythms, two floors of equal height with a fenestration of *demie-croisée, croisée, croisée, demie-croisée.* This clarity and balance of the elevations was made more imposing by the tall pitched roof, which created an extra floor, but when seen from below from the courtyard is less dominant than in a drawn elevation (Fig. 99). Pillars or some other form of simple classical decoration were probably included in the design of the gallery, as personally recommended by de l'Orme as not too expensive an embellishment, and a further affinity of the Hôtel de Donon with the Hôtel de l'Orme is in the limitation of classical ornament to the entablature and dormers of the main block. The entablature of the Hôtel de Donon has de l'Orme's scroll brackets to support the cornice. On the courtyard side the composition of the dormers is unpretentious but sophisticated; the arches of the windows are made up of clear solid masses, pillars, block capitals, broad arch mouldings and projecting keystones. The broad triangular pediment joins

135

the two dormers, but in breaking the base moulding of the pediment the architect artfully gave to each dormer its own cornice. On the garden side (Fig. 98) the two main dormers over the *croisées* are separate with their own pediments, and to echo the proportions of the windows below half size dormers were placed above the *demie croisées* on the left and right of the main pair.

Only where the width was available could systems of columns or pilasters be used intelligently and to good effect. De l'Orme was keenly aware of the unsuitability of the narrower sites on the *lotissements* for the demands of classical styles which required width to be properly articulated. It would be interesting to know if Bernard de Girard had a particular house in mind when he wrote of interiors being made ugly in order to satisfy the requirements of classical embellishments on the exterior. The Hôtel de Donon is a prime example of a town house where the application of classical decoration would have been to its detriment, and which should have pleased those writers of the 1560s and 1570s who scorned architectural fashion.

The next house to the north of the Hôtel de Donon (plots 56, 51, and 52 in Fig. 18), now known as the Hôtel de Marle, has been remodelled on several occasions, but there are reasons for believing that the main part of this substantial house is mostly a building of the late 1560s or 1570s[49] (Fig. 100). On a north–south axis, with a basement, an enfilade of three rooms on two floors of equal height and an attic storey, the *corps de logis* bisects the site between courtyard and garden in the familiar way. In the course of its restoration during the 1960s a false roof was removed to reveal the joinery of the admirable hipped roof 'à la Philibert de l'Orme' now to be seen as it was intended with its gentle ogee profile.[50] The symmetry of the garden elevation has been upset by the piercing of a door and window, the second bay from the left. It is possible that the present plain appearance of the house does not represent the full extent of the intentions of either of the sixteenth-century owners of the Hôtel de Marle, for it can be imagined how the wide, bare areas of wall between the windows might have been filled with two tiers of panels framed by pilasters like the Hôtel du Cardinal de Meudon, or even a system of giant pilasters as Diane de France, Duchesse d'Angoulême embellished an existing *corps de logis* which will be discussed below (Figs 111–114). None of the pre-revolutionary guides or histories of Paris mention the Hôtel de Marle as having a classical appearance. Many of Serlio's and du Cerceau's models show only basic dispositions of plan and elevation, and left decorative refinements as a matter for further discussion between a patron and his architect or master mason.

When De La Noue wrote of houses begun 'with pleasure, continued with pain, and completed with sorrow,' he was prophesying the fate of two, if not of three, of the most interesting Parisian buildings of the late 1570s and 1580s, the Hôtel de Nevers (Figs 101–103), the Hôtel Mortier

100
Hôtel de Marle. Garden front.

(Fig. 105) and the Palais Abbatial of Saint-Germain-des-Prés (Figs 107–109) which were never completed. The builder of the Hôtel de Nevers was Louis de Gonzague (1539–1595), one of the most interesting person-alities and patrons of the arts and sciences of late sixteenth-century France; a serious study on Louis de Gonzague would bring rich rewards not least on Franco-Italian literary and artistic relations. Nevers' secretary was Blaise de Vigenère (1523–1596) a distinguished antiquarian, a philologist, chemist, historian, art historian, the first theoretician of translation and the only contemporary to leave a critical account of French artists of the sixteenth century.[51] The Hôtel de Nevers was the subject of much contemporary comment and admiration, and de Vigenère mentions one special feature of his patron's house, a vault built by men brought from Italy by Louis de Gonzague, which was '. . . aussi platte et plus grande que celle des Thermes de Caracalle, . . .' De Vigenère certainly exaggerated the scale of the vault, but it must have been very imposing and wholly new to Paris. If no record of the appearance of the Hôtel de Nevers had survived, a

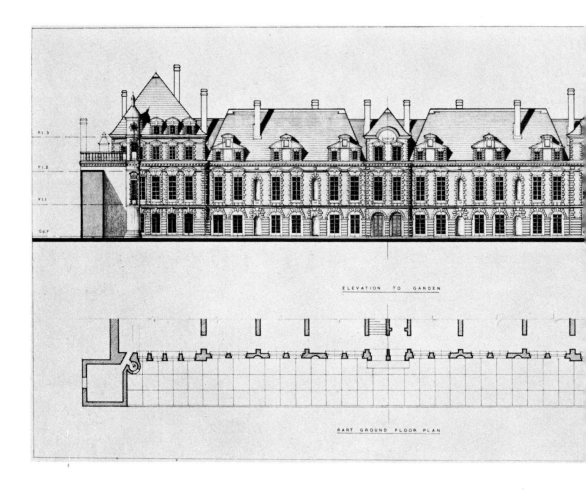

ELEVATION TO GARDEN

PART GROUND FLOOR PLAN

building as thoroughly French in its elevations and silhouette would be thought improbable.

Sylvestre's small copperplate engravings give a vivid impression of how the north pavilion of the Hôtel de Nevers was the prominent feature of its part of the Left Bank. Gonzague chose the site because it was close to the newly begun Pont Neuf connecting the north and south banks of the Seine across the western end of the Ile de la Cité (Fig. 103), and was directly opposite and visible from the 'pavillon du roi' of the Louvre. His intention was to build the largest private house within the city walls, and with the *lotissements* filled by the late 1570s, the availability of the last remaining of the large medieval royal properties, the Hôtel de Nesle, was an opportunity to build an expansive house and a landmark. Louis de Gonzague was not amongst those who bankrupted themselves by building, for his personal fortune was already considerable before he married Henriette de Clèves the richest heiress in France of her day, but the complete project for the Hôtel de Nevers anticipated the full and uncontested title to the whole site and the acquisition of more ground for the south pavilion. Nevers

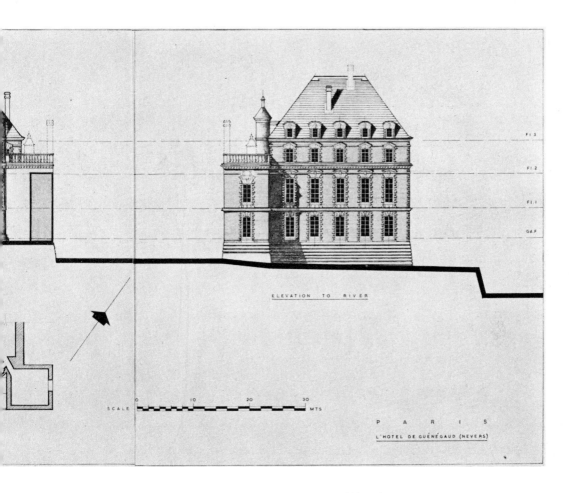

ELEVATION TO RIVER

SCALE 0 10 20 30 MTS

P A R I S
L'HOTEL DE GUÉNÉGAUD (NEVERS)

101
Hôtel de Nevers. Elevation of garden (east) front, and of the north side of the angle pavilion facing the Seine. Reconstruction drawing by A. Don Johnson.

102
Hôtel de Nevers. Gallery, detail of an engraving by Poinsart.

103
Hôtel de Nevers. View of its setting in the mid-seventeenth century. Engraving by Israel Sylvestre.

might have been hoping to see his initiative followed by others building fine houses nearby, to transform a dilapidated quarter of the city. After decades of litigation with the municipality over rights to the walls and adjacent ground, the Nevers family thought of demolishing the house, and were very pleased to sell it with all its troubles in 1642.[52]

Begun by 1582, the architecture of the *corps de logis* and of the gallery at right angles to it on the quayside was of great significance for royal and aristocratic building in Paris over the following forty years, and especially influenced the architectural thought of the avid builder, Henri IV. The *corps de logis* of the Hôtel de Nevers was not the first brick building in Paris,[53] but it was the earliest example in the city of a brick and stone style developed in the Ile de France during the 1540s and 1550s. The name of the architect is not known, but the refined use of quoins points to a Court architect, either the aged Pierre Lescot or more probably Henri III's favourite architect who had been trained by Lescot or who had been his assistant, Baptiste Androuet du Cerceau.[54] Lescot's reputation is based solely on his design of the Louvre, but he was also the designer of the Château de Vallery built from 1549 to 1555 (Fig. 104), which has been singled out by one recent writer as representing several steps forward in brick and stone architecture in France.[55] The probable link of the style of the Hôtel de Nevers with the architectural thought and styles of Pierre Lescot creates an historical *impasse,* for the loss of the manuscript of his treatise with its '. . . plants & pourtraits des plus superbes & magnifiques palays . . .' and the diversity of his style in reliably attributed and documented buildings, at the Louvre, Vallery and the entrance gate of the Hôtel des Ligneris/Carnavalet, makes it impossible to judge or to describe the sources and motives for the use and combination of decorative

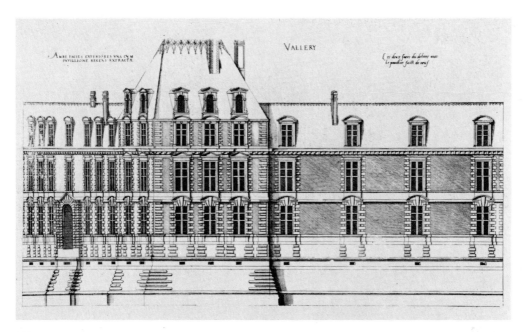

104
Vallery. Outside elevation of the angle pavilion.

elements in his elevations. The proportions of the angle pavilion of Vallery are analogous to those of the 'pavillon du roi' of the Louvre (Fig. 61), but the decoration of Vallery using no order of column or pilaster, with rustication breaking the stone mouldings of the windows and rusticated keystones interrupting the base mouldings of the pediments is the sort of architectural solecism which was inspired by the work of Giulio Romano at Mantua, and it is appropriate that this architectural manner was used for the Parisian palace of a Gonzaga.

The arrangement of the components of the garden front of the Hôtel de Nevers, with its narrow central-staircase pavilion, twin flanking blocks and large-angle pavilions, is a composition of masses typical of French country-house architecture of the reign of Henri III, especially of houses by or attributed to Baptiste Androuet du Cerceau at Fresnes and Liancourt.[56] It was his custom, following the tradition of the châteaux of François I, to give each portion of the elevation an individual steeply pitched roof. As an essay in rustication the Hôtel de Nevers was less adventurous than Vallery, with quoins rarely breaking a moulding, but the architect was obviously interested in creating variety in the design of the decoration for each floor. The ground floor has a blind arcade between the angle pavilions, and there are three different treatments of the tops of the windows and the niches across the full width of the ground floor. On the first-floor curved pediments are used for the *piano nobile,* and above the main cornice the variety becomes more deliberate, with twin dormers capped by alternating broken triangular and curved pediments, their breaks being made by triangular pedimented tabernacles in the curved pediments, and curved pedimented tabernacles in the triangular pediments. Nevers' twin dormers should be compared to those of the Tuileries and that of the Hôtel de Donon. The attic storey of the angle pavilions of the Hôtel de Nevers have quoined windows with only the upper moulding of a shallow triangular pediment, whilst the dormers above are given fully-fledged curved pediments. Pediments are the only decorative motif from the repertoire of the orders of classical architecture to be adopted in this style of brick and stone architecture.

The walls of the gallery were built, but it was never roofed.[57] Its elevation was in complete and deliberate contrast to the *corps de logis*, with giant pilasters supporting alternating curved and triangular pediments. Henri IV was greatly impressed by Nevers' building, and joked that once the house was finished he would be coming to stay. The western half of the Grande Galerie of the Louvre (Fig. 135) across the river imitated the style of Nevers' gallery on a grander scale. The variety and disparity of the architectures around the garden of the Hôtel de Nevers is much in the spirit of de Vigenère's counsels to patrons and builders, such as his view that '. . . l'ordonnance et disposition d'un bastiment . . . dépend de la fantaisie de l'architecte, qui est comme un nouveau créateur quant à la forme et figure'. In numerous comments scattered through his writings de Vigenère argued, in a vein like Vasari praising the creativity of Michelangelo's architecture, that the ancient rules of architecture are of value, but should not be taken as final, that the architect must have a particular talent that goes beyond anatomical knowledge, and that he must transcend conventions in order to invent. De Vigenère placed the talented and original architect at the summit of his artistic hierarchy. Although his urgings of architects to think for themselves, and not to be cowed by rules or by the example of others, are not wholly new in architectural writing, the designing of the Hôtel de Nevers must owe something to his notions of experiment and freshness of approach to architecture.

The example of Nevers' palace consolidated the fashion for brick and stone building, or at least for quoined elevations in the architecture of *haut-bourgeois* and aristocratic town houses. The first fully-evolved example of this influence is seen at the Hôtel Mortier, on the rue des Francs-Bourgeois just west of the developments on the Culture Sainte-Catherine (Fig. 105).[58] The special and only *all'antica* feature of the garden façade of this house is the game played with the pediments over the windows. Vertically, the pediments at ground-floor level start as broken end stubs, above on the first floor they appear as curved without a base moulding and bisected by a keystone, and on the dormers they are full-curved pediments with only the base mouldings broken by a keystone. Read vertically the pediments are progressively completed, whilst on the advanced bays the system is varied and inverted, with full triangular

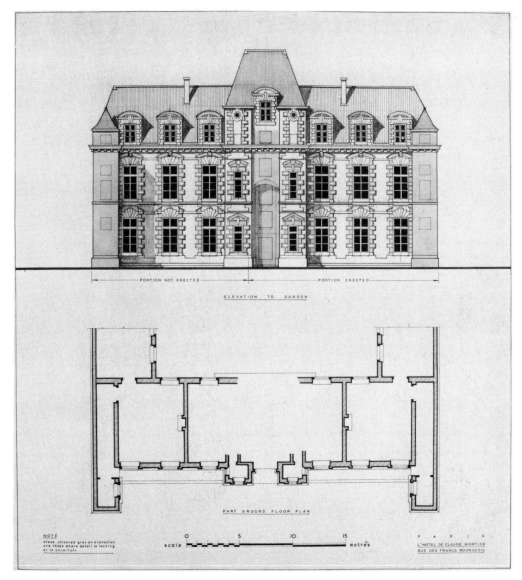

105
Hôtel Mortier. Garden front. Reconstruction drawing by A. Don Johnson.

pediments with broken-base mouldings on the ground floor, fully broken curved pediments on the first floor, and oculi on the attic. In the manner of the ground floor of Vallery, the windows have superimposed quoins.

The date of the building of Claude Mortier's house can only be given as somewhere between 1572 and 1586, but it is probable that the design and building took place during the latter part of the period. Mortier was of the same class of men who had built their houses on the Culture Sainte-Catherine in the late 1540s, a notary and Royal financial secretary.

106
Hôtel de Savourny. View of *corps de logis*. Present condition.

The reconstruction shows the garden façade as it would have been completed, for only the central bays and the four bays to the right were built. The Hôtel Mortier might have been begun 'with pleasure' in anticipation of completing the design on the next plot to the east, but for unknown reasons this fine composition was never more than a noble fragment of a full scheme which would have been as large as any *hôtel* in the Marais. Proof that the Hôtel Mortier was the building 'en vue' in the Marais of the 1580s is found in the contracts of 1586 for the building of the Hôtel de Savourny on plots 59 and 48 of the Culture Sainte-Catherine (Fig. 106), where the mason was instructed to build dormers '. . . semblables à celles . . . de M. Mortier . . .' and the carpenter who was to make the doors for the gateway to the street agreed to copy those of the Hôtel Mortier.[59] Carlo Savornini or Savourny was a royal equerry, and like Gonzaga he built his more modest house in the current Parisian fashion, with a decoration of rustication less refined than the bevelled blocks on the garden front of the Hôtel Mortier, void of columns or pilaster, and without pediments.

The only intact survivor of a building in the brick and stone style from the reign of Henri III in Paris is the Palais Abbatial of Saint-Germain-des-Prés, built in 1586 for Charles de Bourbon, the pretender to the throne

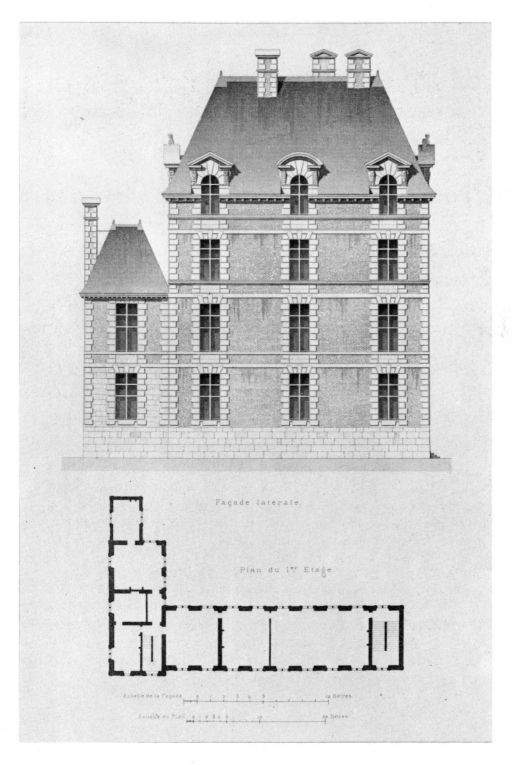

Façade latérale

Plan du 1ᵉʳ Etage

Echelle de la Façade

Echelle du Plan

107
Palais Abbatial of Saint-Germain-des-Prés. East front. Engraving from Berty.

108
Palais Abbatial of Saint-Germain-des-Prés. North front. Photo: Inventaire Général.

during the War of the League as Charles X, and designed by the master mason and architect Guillaume Marchant.[60] Both the outward elevations and those facing the garden are in the rustic idiom (Figs 107–109) and the analogies in its decorative details with the Hôtel de Nevers and the Hôtel Mortier are numerous. Marchant gave the Palais Abbatial an imposing gable for its angle pavilion like that at Nevers, and designed a revised

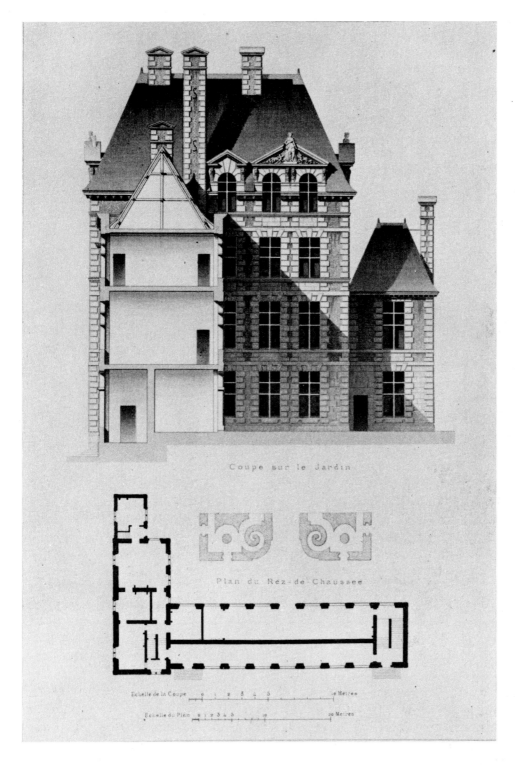

Coupe sur le Jardin

Plan du Rez-de-Chaussée

Echelle de la Coupe   0 1 2 3 4 5   10 Metres

Echelle du Plan   0 1 2 3 4 5   10   20 Metres

109
Palais Abbatial of Saint-Germain-des-Prés. Section and east wing from garden side. Engraving from Berty.

110
Hôtel de Gondi (Condé). Bird's-eye view by Lespinasse.

version of Nevers' pedimented twin dormers which cut and fragment the main cornice in the manner of the Hôtel d'Angoulême (Figs 112–113). Unlike Nevers and Mortier the Palais Abbatial pediments are used exclusively on the dormers, with alternating triangular and semi-circular pediments with broken base mouldings on both sides of the north wing. Looking at the elevations of the eastern block of the Palais Abbatial, it is difficult to believe that the building which we see today, begun in 1586 and finished about 1590, can represent the full scheme envisaged by Guillaume Marchant or Henri IV's uncle Charles de Bourbon. It is possible only to conjecture, but the garden front of the east wing in particular looks like a portion of a longer composition (Fig. 109) with one or two more large pavilions to be added. It was not uncommon for patrons and master masons to sign building contracts for half, or less, or more, of a project agreed in the form of a drawing or model. The sixteenth-century building history of the Louvre is the classic example of this procedure, but such caution did not always lead to the satisfactory completion of houses. As compensation, since its cleaning in the 1970s, the Palais Abbatial of Saint-Germain-des-Prés is the earliest well-preserved building in Paris where the polychromy of red brick and sandstone can be admired, and it shows the style fully developed before its apogee under the auspices of Henri IV with the place Royale (des Vosges) and the place Dauphine.[61]

The story of aristocratic building on the Left Bank during the sixteenth

111
Hôtel d'Angoulême. View of garden front. Engraving by Israel Sylvestre.

century is even more fragmentary than that of those parts of the Right Bank, les Halles or the parish of Saint-Germain-l'Auxerrois, which have been cleared or redeveloped in every succeeding century. Only a small number of the very wealthy and powerful chose to build on the Left Bank, amongst whom were the Gondi who accumulated a large holding to the north-east of where the Odéon now stands. The buildings seen at the left in de Lespinasse's drawing (Fig. 110), showing the considerable additions by François Mansart and Jacques Gabriel for the Condé in the seventeenth century, are thought to be those built for Jérôme II de Gondi during the late 1570s or early 1580s.[62] The narrow central passage and staircase pavilion at the end of the courtyard is of similar form and proportion to that of the Hôtel de Nevers, and the window mouldings show the persistent influence of the Louvre, but the curious, illiterate use of classical ornament on the central pavilion is surprising on the house of a family so closely linked to Catherine de Medici.

Back on home ground on the Culture Sainte-Catherine there stands the lone surviving masterpiece of a truly classical late-Renaissance Parisian town house, the Hôtel d'Angoulême, on plots 17 to 15 of the *lotissement* on the south side of the rue des Francs Bourgeois opposite the Hôtel des Ligneris/Carnavalet (Figs 111–114). In 1584 Diane de France, Duchesse d'Angoulême, the natural daughter of Henri II, bought the property.[63] Before a satisfactory analysis of the Hôtel d'Angoulême can be written, the

112
Hôtel d'Angoulême. Elevation of the garden front. Drawing by Robert de Cotte.

extent to which the site had been developed in the forty years between the *lotissement* and the sale to Diane de France must be defined. It is most unlikely that the fabric of the *corps de logis* is entirely due to the duchess, and it is possible that the extraordinary architecture was tailored to encase a partly or wholly built wing. The garden front of the Hôtel d'Angoulême has been known only through Israel Sylvestre's charming small copper-plate (Fig. 111), but a neat elevation by Robert de Cotte in the Bibliothèque Nationale, which was classed as being of Saint-Maur, shows with precision the proportions and much of the detail of the east front of the house which now stands stark and denuded of its dressed stone architecture (Fig. 112). The garden front repeated the architecture of the courtyard in the giant pilasters and dormers, but the rhythm of the bays has been altered to accommodate a wider central pediment in the attic than that of the courtyard, thus displacing the end pilasters in the junctions of the angle pavilions. Windows on the two sides of a thin *corps de logis* invariably were made to match each other, but they are staggered on the Hôtel d'Angoulême which explains the differences made in the composition of the garden front, and the disparity gives a little more weight to the hypothesis of the architecture on the house having been bent and stretched to fit on to an awkward structure. The garden front has a number of other discordant elements, the most conspicuous of which is its asymmetry. To the right there is a lower two-storey rectangular projecting pavilion which does not wear any of the classical garb of the *corps de logis*. At the almost contemporary Hôtel de Nevers (Fig. 101) a similar pavilion was attached to the right-hand pavilion of the garden front where it served as a

113
Hôtel d'Angoulême. Courtyard front of the *corps de logis*.

junction between the *corps de logis* and the gallery, and it is reasonable to believe that Diane de France's architect intended a gallery along the north side of the garden to screen the main block from the rue des Francs-Bourgeois. The Duchess complained on at least one occasion of the violation of her privacy and the smashing of her windows by undesirables on the street.[64] The method of De Cotte's elevation makes the imbalance in the dormers less noticeable than it would have been to anyone standing in the garden. Omitted from the left-hand angle pavilion of the garden front is the raised attic storey of the courtyard front with its fine screwhead pediment with sculptures of a stag and huntresses, emblematic of the builder of the house. At first sight, it might be supposed that the plain two bay part of the garden front, to the left of the angle pavilion, with its *cabinet suspendu* is a later addition to the house, but the attic cornice is continuous and the tiny *cabinet suspendu* on its elongated column fits with the 1580s, resembling one built on to the château of Wideville of 1580 as an oratory for private prayer.[65]

The east front of the Hôtel d'Angoulême may have faced the garden, but

114
Hôtel d'Angoulême. Pediment sculptures of the southern-angle pavilion.

it was not necessarily the private side of the house. The duchess kept her horses in stables on the other side of the rue Pavée, and so the courtyard had to accommodate fewer services than that of the Hôtel des Ligneris/ Carnavalet or the Hôtel de Donon. The garden was bounded on the north side by the rue des Francs-Bourgeois and on the east by the rue Culture Sainte-Catherine (the present rue de Sévigné). On the garden front was the large imposing pediment and two flights of stairs to the central doorway which in fine weather would have made a more impressive approach for an important guest, and at least one gate in the garden wall existed on the rue Culture Sainte-Catherine on a line with the central doorway of the garden front. The Hôtel d'Angoulême had alternative main fronts.

The architect of the elevations of the Hôtel d'Angoulême can be identified as Louis Métezeau,[66] and without full information on the conditions of the site in 1584 the reasons for his choice of the giant pilaster to articulate the court and garden front can only be guessed. He had to hand Jean Bullant's design of the garden front of the *petit château* of Chantilly (Fig. 115) of the early 1560s which he imitated closely in his use of giant unfluted Corinthian pilasters, the breaking of the full Corinthian frieze and cornice with tall pedimented dormers, and slender projecting angle pavilions with their prominent attic *cabinets*. There was

152

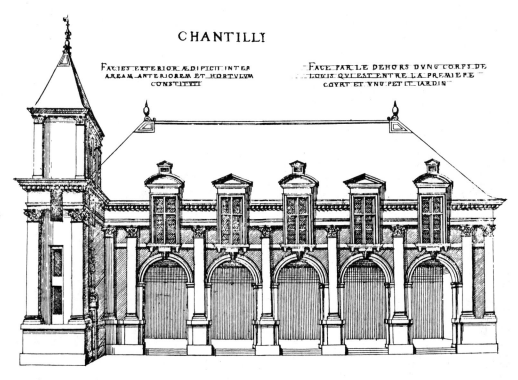

FACIES EXTERIOR ÆDIFICII INTER
AREAM ANTERIOREM ET HORTVLVM
CONSTITVTI

FACE PAR LE DEHORS DVNG CORPS DE
LOGIS QVI EST ENTRE LA PREMIERE
COVRT ET VNG PETIT IARDIN

115
Chantilly. Garden front of the *petit château*. Engraving from *Le Second Volume des plus excellents Bastiments de France* by Androuet du Cerceau of 1579.

also a plate from de l'Orme's book alongside his description of his house on the rue de la Cerisaie (Fig. 116) which is his only attempt to show how a Parisian *corps de logis* might be monumentalized, and he too opted for the giant unfluted Corinthian pilaster. Conventional Vitruvian wisdom would have Corinthian columns and pilasters fluted, and would not allow the breaks in the cornice and frieze made by the dormers. Pilasters were known to have been invented as foils to, or echoes in shallow relief of, columns on the back wall of a portico, but the example of Lescot at the Louvre had created a prestigious precedent. Métezeau's use of the unfluted giant Corinthian pilaster on the Hôtel d'Angoulême ran contrary to Philibert de l'Orme's notions on the use of pilasters on the house of a princess, for in his description of the Tuileries he wrote in Vitruvian spirit that the Ionic order was feminine, which was his reason for choosing the Ionic for the palace of Catherine de Medici. It would have been absurd and costly to use columns on a Parisian town house of the scale found on the *lotissements;* tall buildings with closely-spaced windows naturally suited the giant pilaster.

The Hôtel d'Angoulême has an architecture which reflects the cultural pretensions and status of the builder. The complaints of writers which have been quoted, that men should dress, behave and build in a manner appropriate to their station, could not have been directed against Diane de France, for she was of royal blood. Described as a *gynécée de pudeur* in her funeral oration in 1619;[67] a spectacular order was used on her house to express her importance, although the building was smaller than many contemporary *hôtels* in a more modest architectural idiom, it is deliberately different from the house of a Donon, Nevers or Mortier. In the view of Henri Sauval writing in the 1650s the Hôtel d'Adjacet, built for the Italian banker Lodovico Adjacetti in the 1570s to the designs of Thibault Métezeau on the rue Vieille du Temple a block west of the Hôtel d'Angoulême, was the most beautiful sixteenth-century town house in Paris.[68] Almost nothing is known of the appearance of its elevations, and ignorance of it and of the architectural details of many other aristocratic town houses of the 1570s, 1580s and 1590s precludes generalizations on the currency of the rusticated style or on the apparent rarity of the use of orders. The Hôtel de Bouchage is the only late Renaissance town house in the aristocratic *quartier du Louvre* whose elevations have been adequately recorded, in an engraving by Marot (Fig. 117), and is full of seemingly unique stylistic features.

Contracts of 1586 have been found for the building of the entrance wing on the rue du Coq, seen on the left in Marot's engraving, which name Baptiste Androuet du Cerceau as the architect, working for one of the most colourful personalities at the doomed Court of Henri III, Henri de Batarnay de Joyeuse, Comte de Bouchage.[69] No contract has come to light to give the date or the name of the designer of the most exciting feature of the Hôtel de Bouchage, the gallery opposite the entrance wing, screening the *cour d'honneur* from the stable courtyard behind in the eastern part of the site. Once away from the *lotissements* in areas where houses could not be organized on convenient rectangular plots, the *corps de logis,* gallery and service wing had to be rearranged in unconventional ways, and the architect of the Hôtel de Bouchage had to contend with an irregular trapezoidal site. The south wing which was demolished by Marot to give a view of the main courtyard was the wider of two *corps de logis* on the north and south sides of the courtyard. Baptiste Androuet du Cerceau by 1586 was too accustomed to designing country houses for the men in vogue with Henri III to be a clever architect of town houses. The narrow western entrance wing has the conventional arrangement of central entrance pavilion, lateral arcades with corridors above and corner pavilions, the entrance front of a country house with little vertical classical articulation, only pairs of arches with a pillar 'à la Philibert de l'Orme' on either side of the entrance pavilion. Blank friezes divide the floors with pediments over every window and dormer. The fascination of the Hôtel de Bouchage is the gallery, which can be reconstructed from Marot's engraving and an early seventeenth-century drawing in the collection of the Royal Institute of British Architects by Jacques Gentilhâtre which records the decorative details of the dormers[70] (Fig. 119). The ground-floor arcade is in the most straightforward Serlian taste of curved arches with broad pillars with

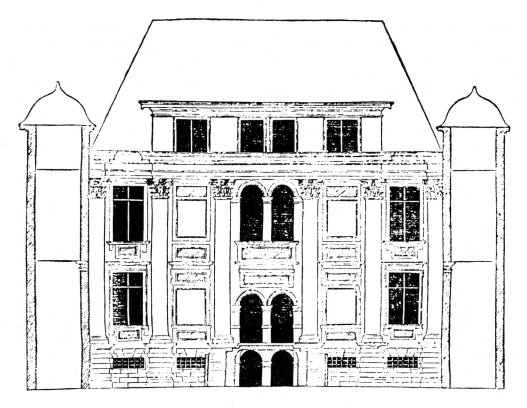

116
Philibert de l'Orme: Design of a *corps de logis* with giant pilasters, from his *Architecture* of 1567.

ground level and mezzanine rectangular openings. The first floor has a system of alternating dormers and niches of unparalleled decorative richness, and is one of the very few compositions in the history of French classical architecture which can be described as flamboyant classicism. In the hoods of the arches of the niches is a plant motif which is made into a fan pattern, and might represent young acanthus plants before flowering with the stems and buds woven into this novel design. The semicircular arches above the hoods are deluged with acanthus leaves from two scrolls in the middle of the broken top moulding. Keystones pierce through all the mouldings to the recesses of the niches, which with their small podia were certainly intended for sculpture, and smoking urns, symbols of immortal memory were put on the top of the keystones. Richly decorated consoles support the triangular pediments over the windows, and the panels between the tops of the windows and the base mouldings of the pediments were probably for mottoes as on Lescot's Louvre. It is regrettable that no record survives of sculpture or inscriptions on the gallery of the Hôtel de Bouchage nor of any intended didactic purpose by the patron. The plainness of the ground-floor arcade would have been a deliberate ploy by

117
Hôtel de Bouchage. View of the courtyard from the south. Engraving by Jean Marot *c.* 1660.

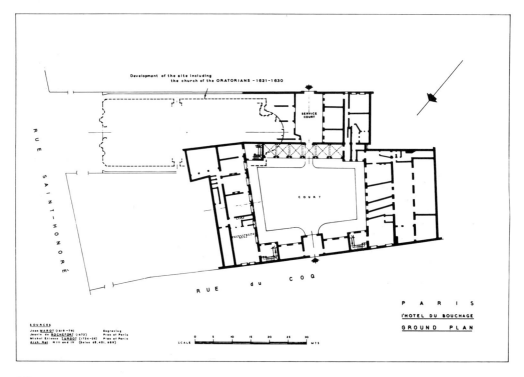

118
Hôtel de Bouchage. Plan drawing by A. Don Johnson.

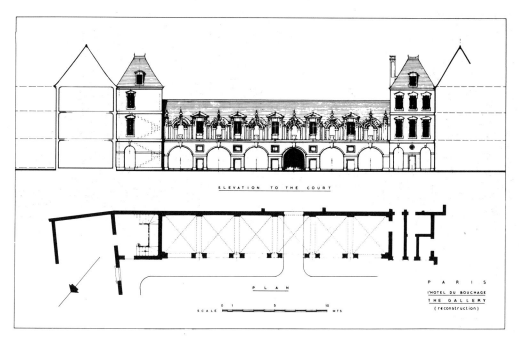

119

Hôtel de Bouchage. Gallery. Reconstruction drawing by A. Don Johnson.

120

Hôtel de Bouchage. View of the east side of the gallery in 1853, during its demolition as a part of the clearances for the rue de Rivoli. (The drawing shows the service court side of the gallery to have none of the elaborate ornamentation of the court elevation.)

157

121
Column from the Hôtel de
Montmorency? One of a
pair of fluted Doric
columns remaining in the
courtyard of a house on the
rue de Braque.

the architect to contrast dramatically with the first floor, where not only
elaborate leaf decoration but also a system of panels and channels cut
vertically between the niches and windows added to the dense complexity
and relief of the bizarre and delightful design. On entering, all the visitor's
attention would have been caught by the gallery rather than by the
intentionally austere *corps de logis*.

During the 1580s in the vicinity of the Hôtel de Bouchage, numerous
aristocratic houses were designed and built by Baptiste Androuet du
Cerceau for leading Court personalities, the Hôtel de Joyeuse, the Hôtel de
Schomberg, the Hôtel Villiquier, but no reconstruction of them is possible
yet.[71] Corrozet's list of the important *hôtels* of Paris written in the 1550s has
been quoted,[72] and a longer list with many more buildings now lost could
be drawn up for the second half of the sixteenth century. Most of the great
country-house builders, the Montmorency, the Guise, the Gouffier and
others less illustrious, had large establishments in the capital and patronized
important architects, and employed leading painters to decorate their
hôtels. The plans of many of these houses are known,[73] but the chance
that a pair of stray finely-fluted Doric columns from the Hôtel de

Montmorency happen to have escaped destruction is not sufficient ground on which to integrate plans and lapidary fragments into a satisfactory account of the evolution of forms and styles in Parisian building (Fig. 121). It may never be possible to write such an account.

3   Households

Life in an upper-class Parisian town house in the sixteenth century cannot have been as regimented as it was to become in the second half of the seventeenth century, when the Prince de Conti wrote down the regulations of his household for all to admire and emulate.[74] He describes a strict daily routine for the buying and preparation of food, the opening and locking of his gates, the education and surveillance of his servants and times for religious observances. Inventories such as that of Pierre Le Gendre describe a house crammed with effects, but is imprecise in defining the use and function of most of the rooms. The French word for furniture, *mobilier,* speaks of the flexibility of most households where reading, games or eating might take place in any of the rooms of the *corps de logis.* An early fifteenth-century description by Guillebert de Metz, of the house on the rue des Prouvaires in the 'quartier des Halles' of Jacques Duchié a clerk of the exchequer to Charles VI, is a glowing account of an opulent and eccentric town house full of unexpected features. It is worth quoting in full, but because of the number of antiquated words which risk being mis-translated, it has been left in the original French.[75]

La porte est entaillie de art merveilleux; en la cour estoient paons et divers oyseaux a plaisance. La premiere salle est embellie de divers tableaux et escriptures denseignements atachiés et pendus aux parois. Une autre salle raemplie de toutes manieres dinstrumens, harpes, orgues, vielles, guiternes, psalterions et autres, desquelz le dit maistre Jaques savoir jouer de tous. Une autre salle estoit garnie de jeux deschez, de tables, et diverses manieres de jeux, a grant nombre. Item une belle chappelle ou il avoit des pulpitres a mettre livres dessus de merveilleux art, lesquelx on faisoit venir a divers sieges loings et prés, a destre et a senestre. Item ung estude ou les parois estoient couvers de pieres precieuses et despices de souefve oudeur. Item une chambre ou estoient foureures de plusieurs manieres. Item pluseurs autres chambres richement adoubez de lits, de tables engigneusement entaillies et parés de riches draps et tapis a orfrais. Item en une autre chambre haulte estoient grand nombre darbalestes, dont les aucuns estoient pains a belles figures. La estoient estandars, banieres, pennons, arcs a main, picques, faussars, planchons, haches guisarmes, mailles de fer et de plont, pavais, targes, escus, canons et autres engins, avec plenté darmeures; et breifment il y avoit aussi comme toutes manieres dappareils de guerre. Item la estoit une fenestre faite de merveillable artifice, par laquele on mettoit hors une test de plates de fer creuse, parmy laquele on regardoit et parloit a ceulx de hors, se besoing estoit, sane doubter le trait. Item par dessus tout lostel estoit une chambre carrée, ou estoient fenestres de tous costés pour regarder par dessus la ville. Et quant on y mengoit, on montoit et avaloit vins et viandes a une polie, pour ce que trop hault eust eté a porter. Et par dessus les pignacles de lostel estoient bellas ymages dorées. Cestui maistre Jaques Duchié estoit bel homme, de honneste habit et moult notable; si tenoit serviteurs bien morigines et instruis, davenant contenance, entre lesquelx estoit lun maistre charpentier, qui continuelment ouvroit a lostel. Grant foison de riches bourgois avoit, et dofficiers que on appeloit petis royetaux de grandeur.

Guillebert de Metz's account of Jacques Duchié's house is the unique adequate panegyric on an opulent late medieval Parisian private house. The description of the architecture and decoration is summary, and although the plan and the arrangement of rooms might be imagined in a number of ways, the listing of the main components and de Metz's characterization of the owner are invaluable. Duchié was not of noble stock, and this 'bel homme, de honneste habit et moult notable' is thought to have made his fortune himself in the service of Charles VI and out of accrued benefices and privileges.[76] In contrast to the disparaging tone of De La Noue when writing of the 'Lawyers and Men of the King's money', Guillebert de Metz looks more favourably on a class whom he calls 'Little Kings in terms of their material splendour'. Once inside the gate, with its interesting device for vetting callers, the house was unashamedly ostentatious with peacocks in the courtyard, rooms full of musical instruments, games, awesome collections of arms, the chapel and most curious of all, the square belvedere at the top of the house with views over the city on all sides, where Guillebert talks of meals being hoisted up on pulleys. It is the earliest mention of such a room. The crowning of the house with pinnacles and gilded figures is the type of spectacular silhouette of a flamboyant Gothic house to vie with a proud Prince or Bishop's residence.

The plans of sixteenth-century *haut-bourgeois* and aristocratic Parisian houses are ambivalent when used in a portrayal of lifestyles and social customs, and it would be misleading to label each room according to its use, as Jacques-François Blondel could do when engraving the great *hôtels* of early eighteenth-century Paris for his *Architecture Française* of 1752–1756. The evolution of the Parisian town house from the Hôtels de Cluny and Le Gendre through to the building on the Culture Sainte-Catherine from the 1540s to the 1580s shows the development of the plan which has been described as 'classic' because of the persistence of its use throughout the seventeenth and well into the eighteenth centuries. The interesting problem is the extent to which this standardization, with all its variants according to the size of the site, can be used as evidence to depict the lifestyle and manners of the Parisian upper classes at home.

The Court's accommodation might have been viewed by a bourgeois or an aristocrat as the model for the planning of the rooms of his house, and as a model for the running and etiquette of his household. The idea of applying the ethics of the formal house, as described at length by seventeenth-century writers on 'the well-run house',[77] to the Parisian *hôtel* of the sixteenth century is tempting, but as one writer has commented, 'The French Court presented a great contrast to the English in that it was, superficially at least, less ceremonious and often more easy-going.' . . .[78] 'Familiarity has never harmed the King of France' was one of the *dicta* of Chancellor de l'Hôpital, and these kings, though they could be magnificent on occasion and never more so when they were in desperate straits, tended to combine far-reaching claims of political and social superiority with personal habits of great simplicity. The King lived in the midst of his nobles.' The function of the rooms of the ground and first floor of the pavillon du roi and the south wing of the Louvre, which were nominally the private apartments of the King, the Queen and of the Queen Mother during the 1580s, were in a building probably not designed and certainly not used for conventional family life (Fig. 59). The room in which the King slept on the first floor is marked 3 in the plan, with the main *chambre de parade* or reception room next door marked 2. It was here that the King would eat, and as a Venetian ambassador Jeronimo Lippomano remarked in 1577, 'During the King's meal, almost anyone approaches him and speaks to him as if he was doing so to an ordinary individual.'[79] The vetting of those allowed in took place at the gate, and the guards in the antechambers, marked 1, seem to have done a poor job in controlling the numbers, which often amounted to a crowd according to Lippomano. The Queen's apartment was in rooms 4 to 10, with her bedroom surprisingly early in the enfilade in room 5, with her *grand cabinet* beyond in room 6. The ground floor of the pavillon du roi contained the King's council chamber, 8, and the Queen Mother had the use of rooms 10 to 13. It is known that the pressure on the royal family at the Louvre caused Catherine de Medici in 1563 to build the Tuileries to the west, where she and Charles IX or Henri III could retreat.

The example of the Louvre shows a flexibility in the use of rooms, where arrangements could and were changed at short notice, and few rooms were used or furnished for a single purpose such as dining. Henri III made efforts in 1574 and 1585 to introduce household regulations which would allow him more privacy,[80] as is described in a letter of December 1584 from Stafford to Walsingham.[81] 'The King beginneth to reform marvellously the order of his house and maketh three chambers afore they come to his inner bedchamber; in the first gentlemen to be modestly apparelled; in the next, men of great quality; in the last, Princes and Knights of the Holy Ghost, with himself when he cometh abroad. Into his private bedchamber nobody to be allowed, unless called in, but Epernon and Joyeuse.' The main shortcoming of limiting the traditional access to the King of petitioners and courtiers was the risk of aggravating the ever present jealousies and rivalries amongst nobles and officials.

No food was prepared within the Louvre itself, but in buildings adjacent to the west to which admission was strictly controlled because of the fear of poisoning. The discovery of an intruder would lead to the dismissal of all the stewards. The royal household and the *hôtels* of the grander nobles were provisioned by a professional buyer or *pourvoyeur*, with the chief steward or *maître d'hôtel* responsible for checking quality and seeing that his master was not being cheated. The contracts for supplies were for periods of one to six years, and the buyer usually was expected to follow the master anywhere within the Kingdom and to sustain stocks of fresh and cooked meats and of fish. Fish from the channel reached les Halles between 3 and 4 am and the buyer was expected to be there, and it would be delivered to the house by 7 am in winter and 5 am in summer. If the chief steward considered the produce to be of low quality the buyer was paid less, and if it was considered inedible the lord's servants would buy in replacements, and the cost would be charged to or deducted from the buyer's monthly or quarterly salary.[82]

The eating habits of Parisians in the sixteenth century were commented on by most visitors to the city who wrote descriptions or kept diaries. Lippomano and Thomas Platter of Basle in 1599, were amazed by the variety of produce available, and noted that Parisians were inordinately fond of meat and pastries. Platter calculated a daily consumption of 200 cows, 2000 sheep, 1000 calves and 70,000 chickens and pigeons,[83] with four to six different kinds of meat being served for a main course. Lippomano gives a vivid picture of how well a man could eat, day or night, if he had plenty of money, but he was surely exaggerating when he lists phoenix as one of the many culinary delights of Paris. During the first years of the reign of Charles IX the city was faced with serious shortages after successive failed harvests, which led to one of the most riduculous of all ignored royal edicts of January 1563. At family celebrations or formal occasions it was to be forbidden to serve more than three courses, six kinds of *entrée* was to be the maximum, and double portions were not allowed. A fine of 200 livres was to be levied for a first offence, and 400 livres for a second, with half the money going to the King and the other half to the judas. Each guest was liable to a fine of 40 livres, and the poor cook to fifteen days in prison for the first offence, thirty days for a second, and a flogging and banishment for a third.[84]

Mealtimes would be regular in the homes of those who lived, worked and were raising children in Paris, but the fractious worlds of royalty, princes or secretaries of state and their families meant that the ideal lifestyle described in the new literature of manners and civility could be of little interest. Henri III's physician Laurent Joubert published a programme for the King's day in which he would rise at 5 am, have a first meal at 9 and another at 5 pm before going to bed at nine o'clock in the evening between May and August. In September, October, March and April the King was to rise at 6 am, eat at 10 am and again at 6 pm before bed at 10 pm, and for January, February, November and December his master was to rise at 7 am, take meals at 11 am and 7 pm and go to bed at 11 o'clock at night, a routine which might have been good for the King's digestion and health, but which he never followed.[85] The inventories of the contents of the houses of the upper classes of sixteenth-century Paris do not help to show where they chose to eat and the earliest proof of a room set aside as a dining room is the *petite salle à manger* seen in the ground-floor plan of the Hôtel Tubeuf published by its architect Pierre le Muet in 1647.[86] The clear separation of the main rooms from the kitchens by a staircase at least, as at the Hôtel de Sens, or further distanced by a gallery, as at the Hôtel des Ligneris/Carnavalet was the preferred arrangement by the middle of the century. Courses might have been served equally well on the ground or the first floor. The cellars of the Hôtel des Ligneris/Carnavalet (Fig. 84) in 1558 after the death of Jacques des Ligneris were well stocked with hard wood and wood for the fire,[87] whilst at the much more compact Hôtel de Donon the cellars of the main block housed the kitchen and servant's parlour.

Brantôme records that François I's notion of a proper welcome for an illustrious guest was the sight of a good-looking woman, and a fine horse and dog.[88] The feminine allures of the hostess and the needs of dogs did not influence the planning of Parisian town houses, but the stabling of horses was a major consideration. Very few would or could afford to keep their horses elsewhere nearby, as did the King and Diane de France,[89] and towards the end of the century and throughout the seventeenth century invariably stables were integrated into the house plan. The size of the stables of houses such as the Hôtels de Cluny, des Ligneris/Carnavalet or Bouchage ought not to be used as evidence of the size of the household, for stalls were provided for the horses of guests and visitors. An *haut-bourgeois* such as Jacques des Ligneris might not have moved about the city on a horse; Louis XII preferred a mule to a horse, Papal legates made their official entries to Paris on mules, and magistrates went to the courts and to the Châtelet on these tranquil beasts, ideally suited to noisy and busy streets. Mules were recommended for the delicate and for invalids, and the visual proof that mules were not disdained by the great is the often reproduced painting of William Cecil, Elizabeth I's most trusted adviser, out riding on a mule, which is not a picture in the grand tradition of equestrian portraiture.[90]

Carriages were rarities in sixteenth-century Paris, and none of the known *hôtel* plans were devised to accommodate one or more of these cumbersome vehicles. In 1550 there probably were no more than three carriages in Paris, one belonged to Catherine de Medici, one to Diane de France, and the third to Jean de Laval, seigneur de Boisdauphin who needed a carriage because he was extremely overweight.[91] Henry IV forbade carriages within the city, and those who owned one hid it, but by 1619 a text reports '. . . it is now one of the principal conditions of marriage contracts to stipulate the provision of a house with a carriage gateway and a carriage for the mademoiselle'.[92] The plans of the *haut-bourgeois* houses in Pierre Le Muet's *Manière de Bien Bastir* first published in 1623 contrast with Androuet du Cerceau's *Livres d'Architecture* of 1559 and 1582 in fitting bays for carriages into courtyards.

The interior decoration of *haut-bourgeois* and aristocratic town houses can be imagined with difficulty. For the seventeenth century there is an abundance of French and Dutch paintings and engravings showing the furnishing of middle- and upper-class town and country houses,[93] not only their bedrooms and reception rooms, but also their kitchens, courtyards, stables and gardens. Many of the arrangements shown in the engravings of Abraham Bosse (1602–1676) might be very similar to those of the previous century, but we cannot be sure. A common form of wall covering was 'natte', a fine or rough woven matting,[94] and the rich had tapestry; in 1554 Jacques des Ligneris ordered 80 measures of Beauvais tapestry for his hall.[95] The finest of French Renaissance furniture is now dispersed in museums throughout Europe and America, and neither at the Louvre nor at the Musée Carnavalet has a room been furnished satisfactorily to reconstruct the decoration of the 'salles, chambres et cabinets' read of in inventories of contents. Few French sixteenth-century country houses contain collections of contemporary chairs, tables, mirrors or tapestries, and only the Constable Anne de Montmorency's magnificent château at Ecouen, which has become the Musée National de la Renaissance, gives a vivid if incomplete picture of the splendours of a richly decorated house. In Paris, the story of domestic life can be told adequately only from the reign of Louis XIII onwards.

CHAPTER V

Later Sixteenth-Century Royal Building

Jacques Androuet du Cerceau dedicated his *Second Volume des plus excellents Bastiments de France* of 1579 to Catherine de Medici, and she would have been pleased to see three of her several ambitious building projects published; Saint-Maur, as it was enlarged for her by Jean Bullant during the 1570s, a grandiose scenographic plan devised by Bullant about 1572 for the approach to Chenonceau, consisting of a large trapezoidal lower court, followed by a forecourt of large semicircular atria linked to two large rectangular halls flanking and dwarfing the original house (Fig. 122). Du Cerceau's two volumes of 1576 and 1579 are replete with royal and aristocratic houses which were barely begun or never completed owing to changed fortunes,[1] and amongst the most astonishing sights for a Frenchman and a foreigner alike in opening a new copy of the *Second Volume* must have been the large project for the Tuileries as recorded by du Cerceau (Fig. 123), which was the largest and most elaborate monarchical building scheme in Western Europe of the fourth quarter of the sixteenth century.

The bloody and turbulent 'Age of Catherine de Medici' from the death of Henri II in 1559 to her own death thirty years later saw.the completion of the western half of the south wing of the square court of the Louvre (Fig. 128),[2] the building of the ground floor of the Petite Galerie on the western side of the Louvre garden (Figs 129–130), the building of a wing of the Tuileries, the conception of connecting the Louvre to the Tuileries with a long gallery along the north bank of the Seine,[3] and the start of work on the Pont-Neuf (Fig. 134).[4] The purpose, and the result of these massive building programmes when completed by Henri IV, was the transformation of the western end of Paris, when seen from the river, into a monumental complex without precedent in France in scale, grandeur and stylistic variety.

The Tuileries was conceived by Catherine de Medici as the royal retreat from the congested Louvre, conveniently close to it just beyond the city walls to the west, with large gardens and uninterrupted views of the river and of the countryside to the south and west. Anthony Blunt pointed out in his monograph on Philibert de l'Orme that the Tuileries as presented by du Cerceau in his drawings and engravings, as a vast palace with three courts of which the two smaller lateral courts are bisected by large oval halls, should not be taken as evidence of the house designed by de l'Orme

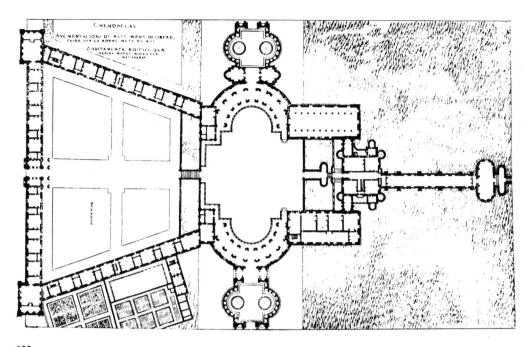

122
Chenonceau. Plan of the enlargements for Catherine de Medici by Jean Bullant. Engraving from *Le Second Volume des plus excellents Bastiments de France* of 1579 by Androuet du Cerceau.

in 1564 or 1565, except for the section of the garden front actually built under his supervision before his death in 1570.[5] (Fig. 124)

In those passages of the *Architecture* where de l'Orme speaks of the Tuileries, he refers to only one courtyard, and to a total of sixty-four Ionic columns on the garden front. When the number of columns on the outer fronts are added up, discrepancies are found between the plans and the elevations in both du Cerceau's drawings and his engravings, and in neither are the sixty-four columns specified by de l'Orme to be seen on the garden side. After much arithmetic by sceptics, Blunt's reconstruction of the plan of the original design for the Tuileries has not been disproved (Fig. 125a); a square courtyarded house with double-angle pavilions at the north and south ends of the garden front, and single-angle pavilions on the corners of the east front, a form of plan which is a variant of de l'Orme's Château-neuf of Saint-Germain-en-Laye and his second scheme for Saint-Maur.

There can be no doubt that du Cerceau did not have access to the arrogant de l'Orme's drawings for the Tuileries, and that the scheme drawn and engraved for the *Second Volume des plus excellents Bastiments de France* is his own proposal, or that of his eldest son Baptiste who was the leading Court architect in 1579, and a favourite of Henri III before succeeding Lescot as the architect of the Louvre in 1578. Twice, during the course of 1578 and 1579, Henri III announced his intention of completing

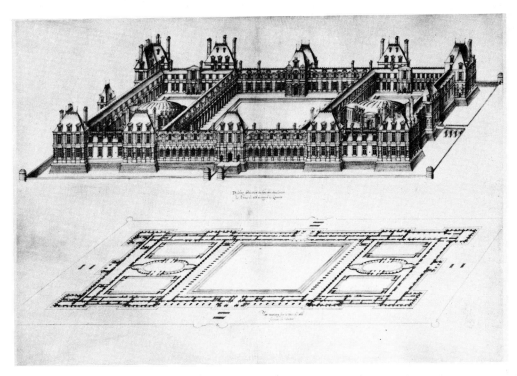

123
Tuileries. Drawing of an enlarged project of 1578 to 1579 by Jacques Androuet du Cerceau.

124
Tuileries. Elevations of the de l'Orme wing. Drawing by Jacques Androuet du Cerceau.

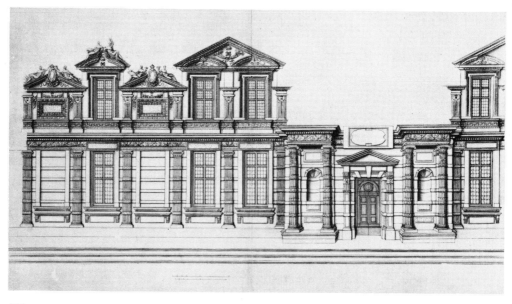

125

Tuileries. Detail of the elevation of the court side of the de l'Orme wing. Drawing by Jacques Androuet du Cerceau.

the Tuileries at his own rather than at the Queen Mother's expense. The lateral courtyards added by du Cerceau are typical of many of his 'multiplied designs', or sprawling houses consisting of multiple courtyards surrounded by one- or two-storey wings with tall pavilions at each junction, which are found in his albums of drawings dateable to the 1560s and 1570s.[6] The wings around the lateral courts and the angle pavilions in du Cerceau's scheme are simpler in the design of their elevations than the richly-ornamented central wing left by de l'Orme. The oval halls in the middle of du Cerceau's lateral courtyards could have been suggested by Catherine de Medici. For two important state occasions and festivals in June 1565 and September 1581 she had built temporary oval structures to house lavishly produced entertainments, and the purpose of oval halls at the Tuileries would have been for the lengthy pageants of dance, music, theatre and oratory which have interested modern historians more than any other aspect of the artistic patronage of the last of the Valois.[7] It is most improbable that one of these halls was intended for baths and the other to house a grotto, as has been suggested in a recent study of du Cerceau's drawings and engravings of the Tuileries.[8] Work on the Tuileries had ceased in 1572, but such an ambitious scheme is in keeping with the pre-occupations of Henri III and Catherine de Medici in the late 1570s and during the early and mid 1580s, when they planned numerous ruinously expensive building complexes in and around Paris designed by Baptiste Androuet du Cerceau at a time when their moral authority and political control over the nation were collapsing.[9]

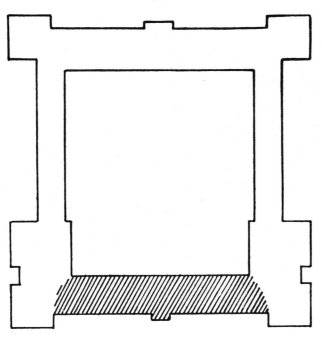

125(a)
Tuileries. Anthony Blunt's reconstruction of the plan of de l'Orme's scheme.

The Tuileries was the most richly-ornamented building designed by de l'Orme, and in the *Architecture* he gave some insights into his thoughts when he had been designing this extraordinary building.

'I will not go on to other matters without pointing out to you that I chose the present Ionic order, from amongst all others, in order to ornament and to give lustre to the palace, which Her Majesty the Queen, mother of the most Christian King Charles IX, today is having built at Paris . . . I wanted to make use of this order for her palace, for up to now it has been used only rarely, and still few people have set it on buildings which have columns. There have been many who have experimented adequately with it in wood for doors, but they have not yet properly understood nor reproduced it. The other reason why I wanted to use and to show the Ionic order properly, on the palace of Her Majesty the Queen, is because it is feminine and was devised according to the proportions and beauties of women and goddesses, as was the Doric to those of men, which is what the ancients have told me: for, when they decided to build a temple to a god, they used the Doric, and to a goddess, the Ionic. Yet all architects have not followed that [principle], shown in Vitruvius' text . . . accordingly I have made use, at the palace of Her Majesty the Queen, of the Ionic order, on the view that it is delicate and of greater beauty than the Doric, and more ornamented and enriched with distinctive features.'[10]

126(a)

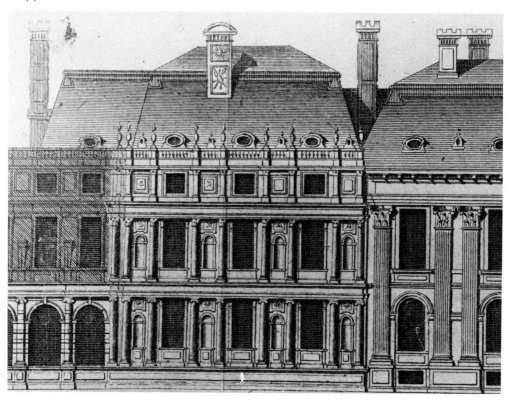

126(b)

Tuileries. 'Bullant' pavilion. Detail of an engraving from (a) Jacques-François Blondel: *Architecture Française*, Tome IV, 1756. (b) Dom Michel Félibien: *Histoire de la Ville de Paris*, Tome II, 1725.

The form of the column shafts of the Tuileries, with fluted drums divided by bands each of which is decorated in a different way, was an invention by de l'Orme of which he was especially proud, and which he christened the 'ordre des colomnes Françoises'. The design, he felt, suited perfectly the stone quarried in France, where high quality hard stone or marble to make column shafts of one piece was not available. This addition to the antique repertoire of five orders of columns was intended by de l'Orme to express the view, often repeated in contemporary Court poetry, that France was the true heir, successor and rival to the cultural achievements of Antiquity. Catherine de Medici intervened with a number of decisions which greatly affected the appearance of the Tuileries; in 1565 when the first drums of some of the columns were set up, she instructed de l'Orme to have them taken down, because, according to the architect, they were not rich enough for her taste, and it was the Queen Mother who required there to be large panels between the dormers for the inscription of mottoes. These panels were framed by de l'Orme with fanciful tabernacles using a curious squat and tapered pilaster form at the sides. The surviving portions of the palace scattered between the Tuileries gardens, the courtyards of the Ecole des Beaux-Arts and the Château de la Punta in Corsica show the columns, pilasters, dormers and tabernacles of the Tuileries were the outstanding masterpieces of non-figurative French Renaissance architectural sculpture. The frames of the panels between the dormers, the friezes above and below the ground-floor cornice, and the plumper drums of the columns which alternated with the fluted drums, are all intricately carved. In the *Architecture* de l'Orme urged his readers to learn to draw and to experiment with decorative compositions of leaves, fruits, small animals and any other motifs which were to be gleaned from nature and the antique. He firmly believed in the thoroughly-trained architect's right to improvise, to adapt and to invigorate the classical language of architecture by using motifs in new combinations and in new contexts. The panel frames derive from the cornices of Roman temples, and the squat tapering pilasters are redrawn herm podia. The free use of various pediment forms in the attic is the most conspicuous display of de l'Orme's spirit of independence, and the aesthetic result of the twin-curved pediments capped with an enlarged triangular pediment above either side of the entrance on the courtyard front has found little understanding or favour amongst de l'Orme's seventeenth-, eighteenth- or twentieth-century admirers. The system of pilasters, and the rhythm of windows and panels of the courtyard elevation is an enriched version of Saint-Maur (Figs 79 & 125). The projecting arcade facing the garden was designed as a pleasant walkway during hot or wet weather, with uninterrupted views across the *parterres* of the long garden and down the river to Chaillot, where in 1583 Catherine de Medici began building 'Catherinemont' as a further suburban retreat.[11]

Slightly later than the first stages of the building of the Tuileries, work was begun on the Petite Galerie of the Louvre, which was connected by a

127
Tuileries. View of the de l'Orme wing and 'Bullant' pavilion, after the fire in May 1871.

tall, narrow passage to the Pavillon du Roi (Figs 128–129).[12] (Sylvestre's view of the Louvre garden gives a greatly exaggerated impression of its size.) In the 1576 volume of *Les plus excellents Bastiments de France* du Cerceau tells us that the Queen Mother by that date decided to connect the Louvre to the Tuileries, and intended the Petite Galerie as the first, short leg of a gallery to link the two palaces,[13] which was to be achieved by her son-in-law, Henri IV, by the building of the Grande Galerie from 1603 to 1606 (Fig. 135). Designed either by Philbert de l'Orme or by Pierre Lescot, who remained the architect of the Louvre in title, only the ground floor of the Petite Galerie was partially or wholly erected in Catherine de Medici's time, the first floor being added and most probably designed during the next reign. The reconstruction of the Petite Galerie published by Adolphe Berty in 1865 shows its condition before the fire of 1660, after which it was rebuilt in its present form with only the central seven of the original eleven ground-floor arches retained. The style of the ground-floor arcade, with its density of crisp, finely-designed decoration, is a highly-contrived mixture of the most 'delicate manner' of rustication, in the bevelled panels which

128
The Louvre. View of the garden, *pavillon du roi* and the south wing. Engraving by Israel Sylvestre, *c.* 1650.

enrich the black marble Doric pilasters and the arches, with correct and conventional classical features in the Doric frieze of triglyphs and metopes. If Lescot was not the architect of the ground-floor arcade of the Petite Galerie, its architect made reference to Lescot's and Goujon's work on the courtyard elevation by filling the spandrels of the arches with figurative, allegorical reliefs. At the Tuileries Philibert de l'Orme's symbolism was exclusively Vitruvian in his use of the 'feminine order' with the prestige of the owner being emphasized in the complexities of the decoration of the elevations. Spandrel reliefs on antique triumphal arches only celebrated the fame and power of the victor, but on Lescot's court front and on the Petite Galerie they are used for a more subtle didactic purpose, to symbolize the cultural, moral and military prowess of a France blessed by the rule of the Valois!

The decision by the Queen Mother to connect the Louvre to the Tuileries was taken before Philibert de l'Orme's death in 1570, and the abandonment of his original scheme for the Tuileries as a free-standing square courtyarded house just after 1570 is proved by work begun on a rectangular pavilion joined to the southern end of the very incomplete de l'Orme wing, which was wholly different in style and out of keeping with the scale of de l'Orme's work (Fig. 126). De l'Orme liked to proceed with building in carefully managed stages, but Catherine de Medici was impractical or ill advised in starting another building to add to the list of her unfinished commissions. The architect who succeeded de l'Orme was Jean Bullant, and the extension of the Tuileries to the south probably was seen as a stage in extending the range of the Tuileries to the river from

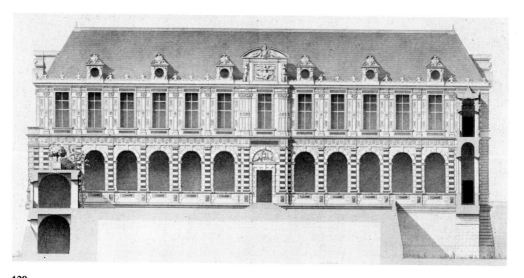

129
The Louvre. Petite Galerie. Reconstruction of the garden elevation before the fire of 1660, from Adolphe Berty: *Topographie historique du vieux Paris. Région du Louvre et des Tuileries.* Tome II, 1865.

where a gallery could be turned eastwards towards the southern end of the Petite Galerie, as was done for Henri IV. Only the height of the ground-floor Ionic order and the continuation of the frieze and cornice between the ground and the first floors across the 'Bullant' pavilion were designed to harmonize with de l'Orme's work. The Bullant pavilion was much less of an architectural experiment or adventure than the de l'Orme wing, with correctly-proportioned and conveniently-decorated Ionic and Corinthian columns. In his porticoes at Ecouen built during the 1550s and early 1560s, his design of the Valois mausoleum at Saint-Denis of 1572 to 1573 or in his book on the classical orders first published in 1564,[14] Bullant demonstrated his allegiance to attached columns as the principal regulator of an elevation's proportions and main ornament. The contrast between Bullant's academic architecture and de l'Orme's work at the Tuileries might be read as a criticism by Bullant of de l'Orme's departures from the example of the Roman monuments, which both had studied in detail.[15] The progress made on the 'Bullant' pavilion before work at the Tuileries was halted in 1572 remains to be defined, but the unconventional forms of the niches between the columns, with their collapsed triangular pediments, and the attic floor must belong to Henri IV's building campaign, when the building was signed with his monogram.[16]

There is no reason to doubt the old tradition that the reason the superstitious Queen Mother abandoned the Tuileries was an astrologer's prediction that she would die in the parish of Saint-Germain; the Tuileries stood within the parish of Saint-Germain-l'Auxerrois, and for the same

130
The Louvre. Petite Galerie. Detail of arcade.

reason she never again stayed at the château of Saint-Germain-en-Laye. In 1572 the focus of her attention turned to the building of the Hôtel de la Reine on the largest single site within the medieval walls in the north west of the city, and her architect for the first phase of the house's development was again Jean Bullant (Figs 131–133).

The two views of the house seen from the garden by Sylvestre and the late seventeenth-century plan show Catherine de Medici's *hôtel* with the considerable early seventeenth-century additions in the northern portion of the site, or the buildings to the left of the central wing in the plan and engravings. The parts of the house built during Catherine de Medici's lifetime are the central and right-hand sections of the garden side shown by Sylvestre. The building history of the Hôtel de la Reine is complex, with more than one major change in the overall conception of the house's plan and elevations.[17] Up to 1576 a design incorporating many features copied from the Uffizi was the approved project, before being discarded in favour of a less ambitious and costly scheme. As built the main courtyard in the southern corner of the site was a slightly irregular square of approximately 30 by 32 metres, with a central staircase in the wing opposite the main entrance on the rue des Deux-Ecus. The tall fluted Doric column, which now has the Halle au Blé for its neighbour, stood in the middle of this courtyard, and its scale in comparison to the surrounding buildings can be judged in Sylvestre's view (Fig. 133); the purpose or symbolism of this strange monument has never been satisfactorily explained. It has been suggested that it might have had some memorial purpose, that it was an

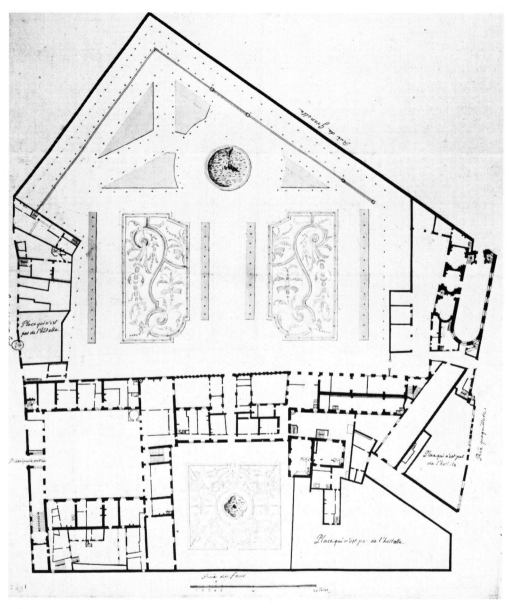

131
Hôtel de la Reine (later Hôtel de Soissons), plan of *c.* 1700.

observatory or served as a watch tower over the city and surrounding countryside.[18] A hall on the left of the staircase was the largest room in the house, and on its north side extended the central wing seen in the views from the garden, consisting of three large pavilions, which were probably designed by Jean Bullant, but were built after his death from 1582.[19] The central portion of this wing was an imposing composition with a large arch filling most of the width and height of the pavilion, and flanked by tall,

176

132
Hôtel de la Reine (later Hôtel de Soissons), view from the garden. Engraving by Israel Sylvestre, *c*. 1650.

133
Hôtel de la Reine (later Hôtel de Soissons), view from the garden. Engraving by Israel Sylvestre, *c*. 1650.

narrow projections of two or more storeys, decorated with pilasters. If the arch was glazed, as shown by Sylvestre, the visitor would have been impressed by the expanse of a costly material. The system of tall pitched roofs over each pavilion created an impressive silhouette for the garden front, and this feature was to be imitated a little over twenty years later in the design of the place Royale. Very few of the architectural, technical and stylistic developments in Paris of the sixteenth or early seventeenth centuries were absorbed from outside.

Judging from the inventory made of Catherine de Medici's possessions after her death in 1589, the Hôtel de la Reine was as lavishly equipped and richly furnished as any of the palaces and châteaux belonging to the Crown.[20] Amongst the tapestries in the house were the famous Valois tapestries, now in the Uffizi, which commemorate some of the festivals and pageants of the 1560s;[21] the house of a Medici would not have been complete without at least one small room decorated in an elaborate and novel fashion, and in the inventory is found the earliest mention in France of a room with walls covered with costly mirror glass.[22] The large quantities of contracts surviving from the sixteenth and seventeenth centuries, which document the growth of the house, are a poor compensation for a fuller knowledge of the appearance of the complex,[23] which was swept away in a large-scale speculative development of the 1760s.[24] Without Sylvestre's attractive but incomplete and schematic records of the garden front, the Hôtel de la Reine could not be included in an architectural history of Paris.

The most durable benefit to the City of Paris from a Royal building initiative of the last quarter of the sixteenth century has been the Pont-Neuf. At the request of Pierre Lhuillier, the *prévôt des marchands*, Henri III appointed a committee of experts on the 7 November 1577 to approve a design of the bridge and to superintend its construction. An early project for the Pont-Neuf, recorded in a painting in the Musée Carnavalet, shows a scheme rejected by the committee before the end of May 1578 (Fig. 134), when the King laid the foundation stone of the bridge designed by Pierre Des Illes and Baptiste Androuet du Cerceau, with seven arches in the northern arm and four arches in the southern arm. The westernmost of Paris' bridges, the Pont-Neuf was always intended as more than a new link between the aristocratic *quartier du Louvre,* and the as yet little-developed western area of the Left Bank. Like the bridges of Rome built by Emperors or Popes, the Pont-Neuf was conceived as a monument of Royal and civic prestige. Neither at the first stages of planning of the Pont-Neuf, nor during the years from 1598 to 1606, when its building was completed by Henri IV, was there any question of recouping some of the cost by building houses for leasing on the bridge, despite the wishes of the City Fathers.[25] The triumphal arches, obelisks and other ornaments shown in the painting were not added to the completed bridge, for once the Pont-Neuf was ·in full use Henri IV's thoughts turned to a new use for the western tip of the Ile de la Cité. The building of the place Dauphine, an isosceles triangle of houses of standard plan built in brick and stone, was completed before Henri IV's assassination in 1610, and was both a profitable measure for the Crown and a practical development which started the process of transforming the western side of Paris into an *haut-bourgeois* area. Before the Pont-Neuf was built, the only direct way across

134
Pont Neuf. Painting of *c.* 1580, showing an unrealized project of the bridge with triumphal arches at each end, obelisks and a large pavilion over the western tip of the Ile de la Cité. As begun under Henri III and completed under Henri IV, the bridge has seven arches in its north arm and five arches in its south arm.

135
The Louvre. The Grande Galerie before its demolition and rebuilding during the 1860s.

the Seine from the western part of the Left B[...]lls
or from the faubourg Saint-Germain-des-[...]all
number of licensed ferries for pedestrians. E[...]of
Valois, the Duc de Nevers was the only a[...]he
transformation of the area opposite the Lou[...]r,
with especially convenient access on horseba[...]of
the city to the east and to the north.

The status of the Louvre as the primary Royal residence in the capital, announced by François I and confirmed by his successors, and the building of the Pont-Neuf under Royal auspices, set in motion the expansion of the western side of Paris by the bourgeoisie and aristocracy, which was greater than the growth of the city in any other direction, especially during the mid seventeenth century and early eighteenth century. The last of the Valois decisively altered the social geography of Paris, and the consequences can be clearly seen in modern times.

Conclusion

Late seventeenth- and eighteenth-century French writers on architecture found much to admire in the treatment of details in the work of their sixteenth-century predecessors, but such writers were little inclined to recommend to their readers the 'assemblage', or the manner of combining decorative forms seen on important Renaissance buildings in Paris. In the annotated 1673 edition of Louis Savot's *L'Architecture Française des bâtiments particuliers,* which had first appeared in 1624, François Blondel wrote

> '. . . the taste of the times in which this author was writing was to crowd the façades of buildings, not only with columns and with pilasters, but also with cartouches, with masks and with a thousand other ornaments composed in strange combinations, and they had not yet their eyes accustomed to the natural and simple beauty of fine architecture which pleases purely through its symmetry or the satisfying relationship of the parts, one to the other and within the context of the whole, and by the correct mixture of suitable and well-adjusted ornamental parts which gives us such pleasure when looking at some of these majestic ruins of antiquity.' [1]

François Blondel (1617–1686) was the first of the Professors of the Académie Royale d'Architecture and the leading exponent of rationalist orthodoxy, and in his published lectures the *Cours d'Architecture* issued in five parts between 1675 and 1698 he insisted that the valid rules of architecture could be learnt only from the study of the buildings of classical antiquity, with the work of Italian Renaissance architects given an honourable second place in his hierarchy. Nowhere in Blondel's copious writings did he recommend his students to study the Royal houses of sixteenth-century France. The little said by late seventeenth-century critics about the palaces and châteaux of the previous century only shows their exasperation with all aspects of their planning and decoration, and which would be condemned or dismissed as 'gothic'. [2]

The most influential of eighteenth-century architectural teachers and critics was François Blondel's nephew, Jacques-François Blondel (1705–1774). In the four folio volumes of his *Architecture Françoise* published in 1752, 1754 and 1756 he argued at length in defence of the French manner in architecture, in which he traced the renaissance of good architecture in the reigns of François I and Henri II, a process which reached its greatest flowering and final maturity under Louis XIV. Despite a more sympathetic attitude than his uncle's towards the work of mid sixteenth-century architects, Jacques-François Blondel could not suppress his feeling that the architecture of a Lescot or a de l'Orme had been a false dawn for the classical style in France. Only with François Mansart, whom he crowned 'God of Architecture', were all of Blondel's requirements of comfort, convenience and decorum fully satisfied, for in Mansart's work Blondel saw the good planning and the fresh, original and harmonious use of classical ornament which were the true virtues of the French national style. Jacques-François Blondel was keen to promote interest, and to elucidate by careful description and analysis, the particular qualities of the French manner as practised by the distinguished architects of the sixteenth, seventeenth and early eighteenth centuries, but where he developed his propaganda into stylistic analyses of individual buildings, he found himself in the invidious position of being both the advocate and the detractor of the Renaissance school in France. Of Lescot's Louvre he wrote both approvingly and disapprovingly:

'. . . This building originally having been begun with the delicate order, and previously only had two floors crowned by an attic, as it has been executed in the greater part of this court, following the designs of Pierre Lescot, who nevertheless ought to have put the Composite order on the ground floor and the Corinthian above, as an expression of the most delicate and the Order which is the most perfect possible for putting on the upper part of the building.'[3]

On the next page Blondel lists his likes and dislikes more fully:

'. . . the defective proportions of the ground-floor arcade, when compared with the diameter of the columns, and with the window openings of the first floor; just as we will be bound to notice many other shortcomings, the smallness of the niches, the multiplicity of architectural members, the returns in the entablature too often repeated, the repetition of the projections, the breaking of the friezes and the architraves, in order to put inscriptions there which cannot be read, the pointless horizontal division of blocks at the wall joints, the oculi which are a foretaste on the outside of the irregularities in the arrangement of the inside, the disparity of the door frames and of the windows which disturb the balance of the decoration, the repetition of plaques and of medallions too poorly arranged, which introduce too many small distracting details, which precludes any domination by the orders which always ought to have the first consideration, and to appear to preponderate over the remainder of the composition. Finally, we shall be constrained to recall the disproportion which one notices between most of the sculpture and the Architecture; so many condemnable discords, and so many break-ings of the rules which show that the Sculptor was not directed by the Architect, and the latter neglected the spirit of propriety, without which one cannot achieve the best results.

'Accordingly, we will pass over these mistakes, and we will stress the admiration which one should have for each of these parts, which are such masterpieces when considered individually, whether for the beauty of such a great number of details, or for the brilliance of the hand which carved the ornaments, which enrich each architectural feature, and which deserve the greatest praise. Likewise, we acknowledge also that it is the genuine beauty of these various parts we would wish had been done with a greater overall economy in the ornaments, and a more general harmony between the whole and the parts. However, despite the irregularities of which we have been speaking just now, there is hardly a building in France more likely to inspire the proper taste in Architecture than the scrutiny of this moment; above all when informed of the rules of the Art, one will be able to judge the worth of each of its beauties, and to make judicious use of them on one's own work; this being the only way of gaining knowledge of that which is truly beautiful, to purify one's compositions, and to avoid the indistinct imitation of the works which have preceded us.'

Many of Blondel's criticisms of Lescot's Louvre are expressed poorly and are difficult to follow. Few can understand his meaning when he states, '. . . The oculi which are a foretaste on the outside of the irregularities in the arrangement of the inside . . .' Modern architectural historians prefer to describe and cautiously to analyse Lescot's Louvre, and Blondel's value judgements would be thought unreasonable and absurd if pronounced by a contemporary critic whose views could not stem, as did those of Blondel, from a living and a developing classical tradition with accepted mathemati-cal rules and aesthetic aims. The problem of Lescot's Louvre, or of de l'Orme's Tuileries, is that they appear to have little context within Western European architecture of their time, and stylistic sources of parts or of the whole of their compositions have not been easily sensed, and never proven. The value of Blondel's strictures and compliments of Lescot's Louvre is that the eighteenth-century critic was fully confident of his rectitude in matters of design and taste, and he was sympathetic to the early classical style in architecture in France. It is almost certain that Blondel was only the most specific of a long line of critics of Lescot's seminal work, which extended back to the sixteenth century. The same points might have been made by '. . . those who are expert in the art find it [Lescot's Louvre] full of errors, both on the outside and on the inside . . .' men-tioned by Blaise de Vigenère writing about 1590. Twentieth-century writers on Renaissance architecture have been neither qualified nor inclined to criticize a building for deviations from Vitruvian pro-

136
The Pavillon de Flore. West elevation. Engraving by Jean Marot, *c.* 1660.

137(a)

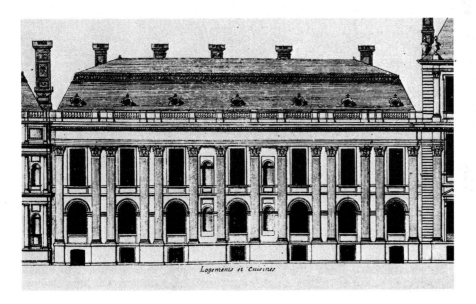

137(b)
Tuileries 'galerie' (a) Henri IV façade (b) Le Vau façade.

portions, or for inaccurate or unclear quotation from antique architecture.

Seventeenth- or eighteenth-century examples of architects quoting from the decorative motifs of Lescot's Louvre in their own designs, or in Blondel's words '. . . judicious use of them in one's own work . . .' are easy to find. The grandiose Hôtel d'Avaux, now the Archives de la Ville de Paris, of 1644 to 1650 by Pierre Le Muet has ground-floor windows, recessed in arches and with mouldings which were copied with few alterations from the Louvre. Lescot's window mouldings reappear frequently throughout the seventeenth and eighteenth centuries on the elevations of *haut-bourgeois* and aristocratic houses. The most interesting example of the reform of a sixteenth-century style by the orthodoxy of the later seventeenth-century is seen at the Tuileries, as remodelled and completed by Louis Le Vau from 1664 to 1666.[4] The 'galerie des Tuileries' built under Henri IV between 1603 and 1606, which connected the Bullant pavilion with the Pavillon de Flore (Fig. 137), had a garden front with an irregular rhythm of 1:2:4:4:1 of giant paired-pilasters between the windows, and had first-floor windows whose pediments broke into the frieze. Amongst Le Vau's 'corrections' was the introduction of an uninterrupted frieze cleared of relief decoration, and he reorganized the pilasters into a symmetrical arrangement. This example of the domination of the orders, unfettered by distracting detail, would have met with Blondel's approval. Above the arcade of the de l'Orme wing of the Tuileries, Le Vau had the dormers pulled down and replaced them with a full storey with an attic (Fig. 126b). Le Vau retained de l'Orme's tapered pilasters on the first floor, a compromise which provoked Blondel to complain that Le Vau was meddling with an imperfect elevation, rather than redesigning it.

Blondel's most persistent complaint is that sixteenth-century Parisian architects did not use a module, the diameters of columns or the width of pilasters, as the basic unit with which all proportions and ratios of a façade should be calculated. On this principle he disliked both the Fontaine des Innocents and the de l'Orme wing of the Tuileries which, he went so far as to say, ought to be demolished to make way for a building in the proper taste.[5] Modular architecture was not a concern of Lescot, of de l'Orme or the architect of the Hôtel d'Angoulême, as it was a preoccupation with Italian fifteenth- and sixteenth-century architects, and which became an ingrained principle at the Académie Royale d'Architecture and with Palladians.

Partly as a reaction against the austerity and stylistic economy of much later eighteenth- and early nineteenth-century neo-classical architecture, many historians and architects of the second half of the nineteenth century admired the idiosyncratic and varied French Renaissance architectural styles without their consciences being troubled by the ghosts of Vitruvius or Blondel. Country houses in the French Renaissance style were built not only in France, but also in England and Germany. This nostalgia did not extend to a critical examination of the development of the classical style in ecclesiastical building, nor to a French Renaissance revival in church building. Individual monuments found their historians, but the churches of sixteenth-century Paris, with the sole exception of the Goldsmiths' chapel, were planned in the Gothic tradition, and their decorations are so unusual and disparate, that an analysis of them as a group has never seemed to be worth attempting.

138
Cloister of the Célestins. Engraving *c. 1790.*

In the 1650s Sauval could count more than three hundred churches in Paris, and of these only four of the largest churches were begun or largely built during the sixteenth century.[6] Sauval shared many of the stylistic prejudices of the Blondels in scorning the application of classical forms to unsuitable 'gothic' contexts. Only in the cutting of some of the Corinthian pilaster capitals could Sauval find anything to admire in Saint-Eustache, the largest of France's Renaissance churches, which was begun in 1532 but not completed until 1632.[7] The most spirited abuse of Saint-Eustache was written in the nineteenth century by Viollet-le-Duc who dismissed it as '. . . a monument which is badly conceived, badly built, a confused accumulation of bits taken from here and there, unrelated one to the other and without harmony, a kind of gothic skeleton clothed in Roman rags and tatters stitched together like the pieces of a harlequin's costume'.[8] Mystery surrounds the identity of the man or the group of men who designed Saint Eustache, and no architectural writing survives from the time of the building's inception to give an insight into the thinking behind this unique and eccentric use of columns and pilasters, and whether it was an unwitting or forced marriage of distinct and unrelated styles.

The only ecclesiastical buildings whose forms allowed for a coherent use of classical ornamentations were the cloister of the Célestins of 1541 (Fig. 138) and the Goldsmiths' chapel begun in 1550 (Fig. 139). The destruction of the Célestins cloister during the first decade of the nineteenth century meant the loss of the most admired Renaissance building in Paris. Sauval remarked: 'The ceilings of the cloister are arranged with great skill. It is the most beautiful cloister; and the good architects do not shrink from saying that it is the finest piece of architecture in Paris.'[9] It would be most interesting to know the names of the 'good architects' referred to by Sauval, and the stylistic features which might be admired by an architect of the generation of Lemercier, a Mansart or a Le Vau. Testard's engraving is the only record of the cloister's appearance, and shows that its form was in the medieval tradition (it was probably rebuilt on the foundations of a fourteenth-century structure), but with the decoration thoughtfully and skilfully adapted. The three principal orders, the Doric, the Ionic and Corinthian were combined in a most unusual way, with giant Doric pilasters facing the cloister walk, full Ionic columns for the outer faces of the piers, and pairs of diminutive Corinthian columns for the arches of the arcade. When compared to Saint-Eustache, begun less than ten years before the Célestins cloister, the stylistic advance looks considerable, and the explanation may lie in the long-standing association of the Order of Célestins in France with the Royal household dating from the reign of Charles V.[10] A contract for the masonry of the cloister of April 1541 has been discovered, which names Pierre Hannon as the master mason for the work, but does not give the name of the architect.[11] On 15 November of the same year Jean Cousin signed a contract for six statues of saints for the cloister, three of which can be seen in Testard's engraving, under the pediment on the east side of the cloister.[12] Jean Cousin the Elder (c. 1490–1560) was the leading native artist of his generation, with a greater range of abilities than any of his fellow painters,[13] and he could well have been the architect of the cloister. The vaults of the cloister walk were of wood, and reports of their outstanding quality strongly suggest an attribution to Scibec da Carpi, who had been established in Paris for at least ten years before the first of his major commissions from the Crown.[14] The Célestins cloister contains few points of comparison with Lescot's architecture at the Louvre, but a common independent spirit in the use and organization of the orders is seen in both buildings, unaffected by the beginnings of the proliferation of architectural books.

Only the façade of the Goldsmiths' chapel survives, and it is in a much mutilated condition, but when fully finished by the mid 1560s, with stained glass designed by Jean Cousin, and with an altar with statues of the Trinity, the Virgin Mary and Saint-Eloi by the eminent Germain Pilon, the Goldsmiths' chapel must have been one of the most impressive small jewels of French Renaissance art.[15] Amongst project drawings for the

139
Goldsmiths' chapel. Façade project.

chapel in the Archives Nationales are two designs for the façade, both of
which consist of three tiers. The drawing which is thought to be the earlier
of the two façade designs has a correct succession of applied Doric, Ionic
and Corinthian attached columns.[16]. The other surviving façade design
(Fig. 139) is a brilliant, original essay in the use of the Doric order in the
context of a tall narrow elevation. Here the architect has avoided the risk of
breaking the classical rules of proportions by using an order of grouped
Doric pilasters on the ground floor only, with caryatids on the middle
storey and panels for the vertical accent of the top storey. This allowed him
to reduce significantly the height of each succeeding tier, which would not
have been possible in a composition using all three orders correctly.
Designed on the basis of simple proportions and ratios (for example the
height from the ground level to the Doric cornice equals the height of the
second and third tiers) this project is a clever and elegant solution to a
problem which had vexed many fifteenth- and sixteenth-century architects, of how to articulate a church façade with properly proportioned
classical ornament.[17] The solution proposed in this drawing is more
sophisticated than any classical church façade in France either before 1550
or of the later decades of the sixteenth century. The design of the
Goldsmiths' chapel as built has traditionally been credited to Philibert de
l'Orme, and no serious objections have been raised to contradict the
attribution. One of the drawings in the Archives Nationales, showing a
section of the chapel, with its architecture of Doric pilasters and panels for
the upper tiers, has an inscription in Italian. It records the writer's approval

140
Doorway design by
Philibert de l'Orme, from
the *Architecture* f° 252.

141
Doorway at Saint-Nicolas-
des-Champs, 1570/1580.

142
Doorway at Saint-
Germain-l'Auxerrois,
1570/1580.

of the use of the Doric 'after careful consideration'.[18] It is certainly Serlio's handwriting, and it is most unlikely that Philibert de l'Orme would have wanted to see his designs vetted by the Italian, which suggests that it was the patrons who were keen to have a good building in a correct classical style, and who sought a second opinion from another Court architect.

Very little can be said of Parisian ecclesiastical architecture during the troubled 1560s, 1570s and 1580s. Important work was carried out on the interior of the church of the Augustins and on the fabric of the Cordeliers during the reign of Henri III,[19] and the small chapel seen in Sylvestre's view of the Louvre garden (Fig. 128) may be the building designed by Baptiste Androuet du Cerceau for the King in 1582. A woodcut from Philibert de l'Orme's *Architecture* showing an arch which he had designed for the festivities at the Tournelles in 1559 (Fig. 140) was imitated on the churches of Saint-Nicolas-des-Champs and Saint-Germain-l'Auxerrois (Figs 141–142). The differences between the woodcut and the doors of Saint-Nicolas and of Saint-Germain cannot properly be called reinterpretations of de l'Orme's design, for none of the alterations can be described as corrections following the recommendations or instructions of another architectural writer of the period. The designer of both the Saint-Nicolas and Saint-Germain doors closely imitated de l'Orme's design up to the frieze, above which a change to a full-triangular pediment was introduced. De l'Orme might have been gratified by the re-use of his woodcut design for two church doorways, but he could not have foreseen that this composition, of relatively minor importance within the context of his treatise, was to become the architectural 'leitmotif' on a monumental scale of the western half of Henri IV's Grande Galerie of the Louvre and of the Petite Galerie of the Tuileries.[20]

The criticisms of later generations of architects, or the wrath of the orthodoxy of architectural teachers, are more likely to encourage instead of discourage a fascination with the distinctive and unique qualities of sixteenth-century Parisian architecture. During the course of the twentieth century there has been a considerable growth in interest in the art of the later Renaissance in Italy and in Northern Europe, and few modern art or architectural historians are persuaded by Wölfflin's notion of the later sixteenth century as a period of decline or stagnation. The use of the term 'mannerism' to characterize the stylistic refinement and iconographical complexity in much Italian, Netherlandish and German painting and engraving, can only be used with very great caution when writing on architecture. The term 'maniera' first appeared in Cennini's *Libro dell'arte*, written about 1390, where he advised a young painter to copy the work of an established artist in order to arrive at an understanding of the technical and stylistic secrets of a master. Over four hundred years later critics and painters of the Romantic period were speaking of 'mannerism' as an excuse for a preoccupation with art and technique in preference to the study of nature.[21] Mannerism in later sixteenth-century French architecture has been more associated by modern writers with excessive use of ornament than with the more significant sense of national artistic and stylistic independence, which can be sensed in Lescot's Louvre, and which is made clear in the writings and in the architecture of Philibert de l'Orme. The spirit of affinity with, but independence from, ancient culture is most clearly stated in the poetry and prose of the second and third quarters of the century.

Joachim Du Bellay's famous *Deffence et Illustration de la Langue Francoyse* was first published in 1549, and part of the special interest of the text is Du Bellay's acknowledgement of the imperfection of the French language in comparison to Greek or Latin. He believed that inadequate or attempted literal translation of ancient poetry could be of little use, or even could harm the reputation of the original texts, and above all could be of little service to the creativity of modern poets and writers. Du Bellay used an architectural metaphor in a passage where he ridiculed the absurdity of those who wished to rebuild the achievements of ancient civilization by using scattered remains, for such an approach to writing or to other liberal arts precluded the full control of the creative intellect and inhibited the development of an original conception.[22] In Du Bellay's view the gifted artist is one who is the master of his erudition, and imitation is a symptom of a perverse use of knowledge. The architects of Renaissance Paris created new styles for Royal palaces, aristocratic and *haut-bourgeois hôtels*, in which each aspect of classical decorative design was thought out afresh. It is not possible to estimate when the feeling arose that a classical architectural manner should be encouraged and developed in France which would be a distinctive national style. In creating a French order for the Tuileries in the early 1560s, de l'Orme certainly was not the instigator of a revised language of architecture or national style. The virtues of the French manner as described by Jacques-François Blondel were based on functional practicability and stylistic restraint and harmony. The mid sixteenth-century pioneers of new classical styles cannot be blamed for ignorance of architectural orthodoxy, in an age when such concepts hardly existed in any of the important artistic centres. The great variety of Parisian Renaissance architecture makes the interpretation of these buildings a part of a wider insight into a society in the process of profound social, political and cultural change.

Notes

Introduction

1 See L. A. Bosseboeuf: *Dix ans à Tours sous Louis XI,* Tours 1890. Louis XI's preferred residence was Plessis-lès Tours, just outside the city, see François Gébelin: *Les Châteaux de la Loire,* édition nouvelle, Paris 1957, pp. 36–40. Louis was referred to locally as the 'Maire de Tours'. In English there is Paul Murray Kendall: *Louis XI,* London 1971.

2 See Adolphe Berty: *Topographie Historique du Vieux Paris. Région du Louvre et des Tuileries,* Tome I, 2nd edition, Paris 1885, p. 202 for the text, where the King states '. . . nostre intention est de doresnavant faire la plus part de nostre demeure et séjour en nostre bonne ville de Paris et alentour plus qu'en aultre lieu du royaulme; cognoissant nostre chastel du Louvre estre le lieu plus commode et à propos pour nous loger; à ceste cause, avons délibéré faire réparer et mettre en ordre ledict chastel, . . .'

3 For François I's building accounts see Léon de Laborde: *Les Comptes des Bâtiments du Roi (1528–1571),* 2 vols, Paris 1877–1880.

4 On the *lotissement* of the Hôtel de Flandre see Maurice Dumolin: *Etudes de Topographie Parisienne,* Tome II, Paris 1930, pp. 341–400, and on the *lotissement* of the Hôtel Saint-Pol see Léon Mirot: 'La Formation et le Démembrement de l'Hôtel Saint-Pol, à propos d'un plan aux Archives Nationales', in *La Cité, Bulletin Trimestriel de la Société Historique et Archéologique du IVᵉ Arrondissement de Paris,* 1916, pp. 269–319.

5 On the final establishment of Paris as capital in the twelfth century see Robert Henri Bautier: 'Quand et comment Paris devint capitale', in *Bulletin de la Société de l'Histoire de Paris et de l'Ile de France,* 1979, pp. 11–46.

6 See Jacques Androuet du Cerceau: *Le Second Volume des plus excellents Bastiments de France,* Paris 1579, fᵒ 3 verso.

7 See Félix Herbet: *L'Ancien Fontainebleau,* Fontainebleau 1912, and Maurice Roy: 'Quelques hôtels de Fontainebleau au XVIᵉ siècle', in his *Artistes et Monuments de la Renaissance en France,* Tome II, Paris 1934.

Chapter I

1 Gilles Corrozet: *Les Antiquitez et Singularitez de Paris, ville capitale du Royaume de France,* Paris 1550, fᵒ 199 recto. Corrozet then lists forty-three monuments, town houses and palaces which he considered to be the most interesting or prominent in the city. Those buildings whose appearance is known in whole or in part, as survivals or from visual records, are asterisked in the transcription of Corrozet's list below; the total is a maximum of thirteen out of forty-three listed. A close study of eighteenth- and early nineteenth-century topographical drawings and engravings would add to our knowledge of the buildings of Gothic Paris.

L'hostel du Roy derriere le Palais★
Le chasteu du Louvre★
La Bastille★
les Tournelles
L'hostel de Nesle★
L'hostel de Bourbon★
L'hostel de Flandre
L'hostel d'Artois & Bourgogne★
L'hostel de la Royne
L'hostel Sainct Paul
L'hostel de Bretaigne
L'hostel de Graville
L'hostel de Clichon★
L'hostel d'Orléans à S. Marceau
L'hostel de Vendosme
L'hostel de Langres
L'hostel de Bavieres
L'hostel d'Anjou
L'hostel d'Albret
L'hostel de Lorraine★
L'hostel de Nevers
L'hostel d'Alençon
L'hostel de Sens★
L'hostel de Reims
L'hostel de Clugny (Cluny)★
L'hostel de sainct Denis
L'hostel d'Auxerre
L'hostel de Laon

L'hostel de Barbou
L'hostel de Lion
L'hostel de Fescamp★
L'hostel d'Evreux
L'hostel de Tison★
L'hostel de Beauvais
L'hostel de Bourges
L'hostel de la Cousture
L'hostel de Rouen
L'hostel de Savoisy
L'hostel de Clermont
L'hostel des Ursins★
L'hostel des Savonniers
L'hostel de Chaalons

2 Gilles Corrozet: *Les Blasons domestiques,
   contenantz la décoration d'une maison
   honneste, et du mesnage estant en icelle:
   Invention joyeuse et moderne*, Paris 1539.

3 The most thorough life of Serlio is still
   William Bell Dinsmoor: 'The Literary
   Remains of Sebastiano Serlio', in *The
   Art Bulletin*, 1942, pp. 55–91 and
   pp. 115–154. Serlio's two manuscripts
   of the 'true' sixth book on domestic
   architecture have been published in
   facsimile with commentaries. See Myra
   Nan Rosenfeld: *Sebastiano Serlio On
   Domestic Architecture. Different Dwellings
   from the Meanest Hovel to the Most Ornate
   Palaces. The Sixteenth Century
   Manuscript of Book VI in the Avery
   Library of Columbia University*, New
   York 1978, and Marco Rosci: *Il Trattato
   di architettura de Sebastiano Serlio*,
   (vol. 1.), *Sesto libro delle habitatione di
   tutti li gradi degli homini*, (vol. 2), Milan
   1967. The researches of Monsieur
   François Charles James on Serlio's
   career in France have been fruitful.

4 Rosenfeld, op. cit. above note 3, p. 63,
   for the full quotation of Serlio's idea of
   '. . . discordia concordante: . . .'

5 The best-known example of this is a
   pronouncement by Marie de'Medici,
   reported as: 'Sa Majesté ne voulant pas
   qu'il fasse cuisine dans son château,
   pour être chose trop déshonneste et
   indigne du respect que l'on lui doit
   porter.' A regulation of 1585 explained
   why kitchens must be outside the
   Louvre. See Louis Batiffol: *La Vie
   Intime d'une Reine de France au XVIIᵉ
   siècle. Marie de'Médicis*, Paris 1931,
   vol. 1, p. 162 and note 1.

6 For the text of the edict see Louis
   Hautecoeur: *Histoire de l'Architecture
   classique en France*, Tome I, ii, Paris
   1965, p. 204 note 7. See also Micheline

Baulant: Le Salaire des ouvriers du
bâtiment à Paris de 1400 à 1726, in
Annales, économies, sociétés, civilisations,
26, 1971, pp. 463–483.

7 See Maurice Roy: *Artistes et Monuments
   de la Renaissance en France*, Tome I, Paris
   1929, 'Les Travaux de Philibert de
   l'Orme à Paris, 1546–1559',
   pp. 348–374.

8 *Catalogue des Actes de François I*, 10 vols,
   Paris 1887 1908, IV, n° 13355.

9 See Maurice Dumolin: *Etudes de
   Topographie Parisienne*, Tome III, Paris
   1931, 'Le Lotissement de la Culture
   Sainte Catherine et l'Hôtel Carnavalet',
   pp. 289–392.

10 Robert Dallington (1561–1637):
   *A Method for Travell, showed by taking
   the view of France as it stoode in the yeare of
   our Lord 1598*, London n.d., p. 17.
   Dallington was quoting extensively
   from De La Noue: *Discours Politiques et
   Militaires*, Basle 1587, of which an
   English translation appeared in the
   same year. De La Noue made some
   interesting observations on building as
   a vanity, see *Discours*, pp. 164–166.

11 On the quarrel between the Prior and
   the monks over their incomes, which
   broke out around 1553 and dragged on
   until 1572, see Dumolin, op. cit. above
   note 9, p. 304.

12 The text was first published by Le
   Roux de Lincy: *Recherches sur Jean
   Grolier sur sa vie et sa bibliothèque*, Paris
   1866, pp. 348–354. 'Lettres Patentes et
   commission du Roy pour vendre et
   aliener à perpétuité son hostel des
   Tournelles et d'Angoulesme, assis à
   Paris, rue Sainct Anthoine.' The most
   interesting extracts are the following:
   '. . . Et neantmoins seroyent fort
   propres, utiles et convenables à bastir et
   edifier plusieurs beaux logis, maisons et
   demeures fort necessaires pour y retirer
   un bon nombre et multitude de peuple,
   qui afflue de jour en jour, et vient
   habiter en nostre dicte ville, dont la
   plupart sont contraincts faire maisons et
   bastimens hors le tour et enclos d'icelle,
   pour n'y pourvoir plus trouver place à
   bastir.
   '. . . (to be sold) à la charge de y faire
   bastir et edifier maisons et manoirs
   habitables, commodes et convenables
   pour la decoration de nostre ville, selon
   les pourtraicts et devis que en ferons
   pour ce faire.'

'. . . faire mesurer et toiser par maistre Jean de Lorme, maistre general de nos oeuvres de maçonnerie, et autrres maistres maçons et charpentiers, nostredict hostel des Tournelles, celuy d'Angoulesme, et tout ce qui en depend, le tout diviser et separer par rues et par places, de telle longeur et largeur qu'ils verront estre requis pour bastir maisons uniformes, et semblables, si possible estre; faire aussi arrester le patron et devis du fronc sur rue chascune desdictes maisons. et priser et estimer chascune desdictes places ainsi séparées: . . . Que icelles places sont à vendre, bailler et delivrer aux plus offrans et derniers encherisseurs: à la charge de les bastir dedans deux ans selon le dict pourtraict et devis qui en aura esté faict, . . .'

13 See Maurice Dumolin, op, cit. above note 9, Tome II, 'L'Enceinte des Fossés Jaunes et la formation du Quartier Richelieu', pp. 111–340, especially p. 114.

14 Noël du Fail (c.1520–1591) in his *Les baliverneries et les contes d'Eutrapel* satirized Jean de Laval, who during the first years of the reign of François I, assembled at Châteaubriant all the great craftsmen of France '. . . illec mandez qui n'avaient en bouche que frontispices, piedestals, obélisques, coulonnes, chapitaux, frises, soubassemens . . .' Although du Fail's text is mocking and exaggerates the number of men consulted and their limited outlook on life, it is evidence of a practice where a patron would seek a range of technical and stylistic advice before building, as recommended by most of the architectural treatises.

15 Sixteenth-century Parisian inventories are often summary in their descriptions of collections of books but, for example, the inventory of the Royal secretary and collector Jacques Perdrier of 19 July. 1578 is rich in architectural books including Alberti, Serlio, Cataneo, de l'Orme &c. See Hélène Michaud: *La Grande Chancellerie et les écritures royales au XVIe siècle,* Paris 1967, p. 185.

16 For a discussion of Serlio, Lescot and the Louvre see below our chapter on 'Municipal and Royal building'.

Chapter II

1 On the Hôtel de Sens see Charles Sellier: *Anciens Hôtels de Paris,* Paris 1910, pp. 289–354. On the Hôtel de Cluny see Charles Normand: *L'Hôtel de Cluny,* Paris 1888 and François de Montremy: 'Le lieu dit les Thermes et l'hôtel de Cluny', in *Paris et Ile de France. Mémoires publiés par la Fédération des Sociétés Historiques et Archéologiques de Paris et de l'Ile de France,* Tome VII, 1955, pp. 53–148.

2 Sellier, op. cit. above note 1, p. 294.

3 J. A. Piganiol de la Force: *Description historique de la Ville de Paris,* Paris 1765, Tome IV, p. 296. On the Hôtel de Sens see articles by Lucien Lambeau in *Procès-verbaux de la Commission du Vieux Paris,* 1908, pp. 188–193, 1911, pp. 188–201, and by Marcel Poëte, ibid, 1917, pp. 136–138.

4 See Geneviève Souchal: 'Le Mécénat de la Famille d'Amboise', in *Bulletin de la Société des Antiquaires de l'Ouest,* 1976, pp. 485–526 and pp. 567–612, especially pp. 569–571, where Jacques d'Amboise is credited with the entire building of the house, rather than the completion of one begun earlier by Jean de Bourbon. Geneviève Souchal has pointed out for the first time the breadth and scope of Jacques d'Amboise's building initiatives at Cluny and at Clermont Ferrand. The palace built by d'Amboise at Cluny (now the Hôtel de Ville) at the same time as his Parisian house is wholly Gothic in style, except for decoration on the east front where there is decorative tracery in a distinctively Florentine Renaissance style, added about 1505–1510. Jacques d'Amboise's architectural and sculptural works at the Cathedral of Clermont Ferrand, initiated in 1507, were wholly Renaissance in style, pointing to the mid 1500s as the watershed between the Gothic and 'Italianism' in the patronage of the d'Amboise. On the palace at Cluny see Kenneth John Connant: *Cluny, Les églises et la maison du Chef d'Ordre,* Mâcon 1968, pp. 128–129, and for a bibliography on the Cathedral of Clermont Ferrand see Geneviève Souchal, p. 573, note 211.

5 On Georges d'Amboise see Louis Le Gendre: *Vie du Cardinal Georges d'Amboise, premier ministre de Louis XII,* Rouen 1724.

6 Anthony Blunt: *Art and Architecture in France 1500–1700*, Harmondsworth 1970, p. 8.

7 See A. Deville: *Comptes de dépenses de la construction du château de Gaillon, publiés d'après les registres manuscrits des trésoriers du Cardinal d'Amboise*, Paris 1851, and Elisabeth Chirol: *Un premier foyer de la Renaissance en France. Le Château de Gaillon*, Paris 1952.

8 See *Le Palais de Justice de Rouen. Ouvrage collectif publié par les soins du Ministère de la Justice et du Département de la Seine Maritime*, Rouen 1977, especially chapter II, 'Construction du Palais de Neuf Marché et du Palais Royal', 1499–1531, by Elisabeth Chirol and Daniel Lavallé, pp. 23–95.

9 See the engravings of the elevations of the house published by Charles Normand, op. cit. above note 1, pp. 123–124 which show how extensive was the restoration and the remodelling carried out by Albert Lenoir, especially in the completely new attic balustrade and the new window piercings in the wing between the gallery and the main-stair tower.

10 I am grateful to Mrs Mary Whiteley for letting me read two of her articles on French staircases in advance of their publication amongst volumes of papers given at colloquiums at the Centre d'Études supérieures de la Renaissance at Tours.

11 See Henri Sauval: *Histoire et Recherches des Antiquités de Paris*, Paris 1724, Vol. II, pp. 11–25, and the article by Mrs Mary Whiteley to be published in French, ' "La Grande Vis": Its development in France from the mid-fourteenth to the mid-fifteenth centuries.'

12 See Geneviève Souchal, art. cit. above note 4, p. 489, note 6.

13 See André Chastel and others: Les vestiges de l'Hôtel Le Gendre et le véritable Hôtel de la Trémouïlle, in *Bulletin Monumental*, 1966, pp. 129–165, and Dominique Hervier: Paris, l'Hôtel Le Gendre dit la Trémouïlle, in *Viollet le Duc* (Exhibition catalogue, Grand Palais), Paris 1980, pp. 90–95.

14 Cf. Dominique Hervier: *Pierre Le Gendre et son inventaire après décès. Etude historique et méthodologique*, Paris 1977.

Madame Hervier generously shared her special knowledge of Le Gendre, and made the interesting point that his fortune and most of his fine possessions must have come through his very advantageous marriage to Charlotte Briçonnet.

15 Cf. Dominique Hervier, op. cit., p. 37 of text section.

16 Cf. Dominique Hervier, op. cit., p. 29 of the transcription of the inventory.

17 Cf. Louis Hautecoeur: *Histoire de l'Architecture classique en France*, Tome I, i, Paris 1963, pp. 134–139.

18 Madame Hervier, in her unpublished thesis, makes a number of interesting comparisons of the decorative elements of the Hôtel Le Gendre with nearly contemporary work at Bourges and in Normandy, and I can do no better than to quote her perceptive text.
'Qu'il suffise de dire que l'hôtel construit dans les toutes premières années du XVIᵉ siècle par Pierre Le Gendre nous semble s'apparenter aux demeures flamboyantes. Son décor, par contre, de quelques années postérieur peut être au début du gros oeuvre, est infiniment plus novateur et rélève, à notre sens, un certain nombre de parentés de la première renaissance.
Tout d'abord, sur des structures encore gothicisantes (arcades des galeries, gâbles des fenêtres) on voit apparaître des éléments de la première renaissance. Ainsi, une des deux colonnes qui soutiennent la tourelle Sud Ouest (Fig. 37) présente un fût ornée de tores en spirale comme on en voit à l'église.
Saint-Séverin à Paris, ou au pilier du Dauphin de la Cathédrale de Gisors, mais elle est surmontée d'un chapiteau très composite dont le sujet mythologique évoque Hercule enfant étranglant des serpents. Ce parti, nous l'avons retrouvé à l'hôtel Lallemant, à Bourges, et sur les colonnettes de certaines clôtures des chapelles du choeur de l'abbaye bénédictine de Fécamp. Ces clôtures sont d'une date plus tardive que le décor de l'hôtel le Gendre mais on ignore, soulignons le, dans quels chantiers a travaillé Jean Brasseur avant d'être employé à Fécamp.
Toujours dans le même esprit, une console, aujourd'hui placée sur le mur sud de la cour de l'Ecole des

197

Beaux Arts, offre la juxtaposition de feuillage flamboyant très découpé et d'un motif de rinceaux encadrant une tête d'angelot. Si l'on rapproche ce motif de certains détails sculptés des boiseries des stalles de Gaillon, le traitement très voisin des rubans plats incisés issus de feuillage et disposés symétriquement par rapport à un motif central, celui de la figure poupine de l'angelot se détachant sur les ailes effilées fait songer sinon à la même main, du moins à un atelier très proche. Or, les rouennais commençant à travailler à Gaillon à partir de 1506, Colin Castile passe le marché pour les stalles en 1508. C'est toujours des stalles de Gaillon, mais cette fois pour un motif très gothicisant, que nous rapprocherons le vestige d'un bandeau sculpté de l'hôtel le Gendre: même façon de lover l'animal dans l'espace qui lui est imparti, même traitement de l'épine dorsale, même manière de ponctuer les indentations du remplage de petits motifs végétaux.

Un autre rapprochement nous a semblé significatif. La partie supérieure du portail monumental sur la rue de l'hôtel le Gendre (Fig. 32) comporte un motif bien caractéristique; celui du feuillage se recourbant sur une boule formée de nombreux grains (déformation de la grenade ou d'un autre fruit exotique?). Or, ce motif est une des caractéristiques de l'ornementation à Gaillon. De nombreux exemples figurent sur les vestiges de ce château.

Enfin, pour une dernière comparaison, c'est à l'hôtel Lallemant, à Bourges qu'il faut retourner. N'est ce pas un esprit très voisin qui a conçu le profil d'homme sculpté au bas de la tourelle et celui qui meuble l'écoinçon de droite du portail de l'hôtel le Gendre? Certes il faut reconnaître à Bourges une habilité plus grande. Le profil de la rue des Bourdonnais dénote une certaine naïveté, révèle un profil plus médiéval qu'antiquisant.

Toutefois, c'est dans la chapelle de l'hôtel Lallemant, à propos du décor sculpté de sa crédence, que certains rapprochements se sont imposés à nous avec le plus d'évidence. Nous y retrouvons comme à l'hôtel Le Gendre un beau motif de lumachelles: à Bourges il délimite le tracé de la niche, à Paris il détermine les écoinçons du portail. Nous y retrouvons également le motif du feuillage recourbé sur le fruit et les rubans incisés placé de part et d'autre d'un motif central (motif sculpté sous la crédence elle même). Nous pouvons encore rapprocher le traitement des oves qui bordent la partie inférieure de la crédence de celui du portail de la rue des Bourdonnais, exactement semblable. Mais il y a plus: le fronton en plein cintre qui surmonte la crédence est souligné par un beau motif de disques enfilés, appelés par les italiens 'nastri a treccia'. Or, ce motif se voit également sur les clôtures de Fécamp. Dans l'état actuel des connaissances, il est difficile d'aller plus loin et d'affirmer qu'il y a eu des rapports entre les chantiers normands, Bourges et l'hôtel le Gendre à Paris. Aucune étude récente ne vient préciser la chronologie de l'hôtel Lallemant ni éclaircir les influences qu'a pu exercer ou subir cet édifice.'

19 All that can be shown are in Figs 52 and 72.

20 See Jean Louis Bourgeon: L'Ile de la Cité pendant la Fronde, in *Paris et Ile-de-France, Mémoires publiés par la Fédération des Sociétés historiques et archéologiques de Paris et de l'Ile-de-France,* Tome XIII, 1962, pp. 23–144.

21 Cf. A. J. V. Parent Duchâtelet: *De la prostitution dans la Ville de Paris considerée sous le rapport de l'hygiène publique, de la morale et de l'administration,* 2 vols, Paris 1836, I, p. 302.

22 Cf. Louis Batiffol: *Jean Jouvenal des Ursins, prévôt des marchands de la Ville de Paris (1360–1431),* Paris 1894.

23 Anonymous French School sixteenth century, Procession of the League on the Place de Grève. Anonymous French School seventeenth century, Sainte Geneviève. A view of the north and east banks of the Ile de la Cité by Jean Baptiste Raguenet (1715–1793).

24 See Louis Batiffol: L'origine italienne des Juvenal des Ursins, in *Bibliothèque de l'Ecole des Chartes,* 1893, pp. 693–717.

25 Cf. Paul de Beauchêne: *La Maison de Racine et la rue Visconti,* Paris 1933, p. 84.

26 See Jean-Pierre Babelon, (summary of his lectures), in *Ecole pratique des Hautes Etudes. IVe section. Annuaire.*, 1972/1973, pp. 501–508.

27 Cf. Henri Sauval: *Histoire et recherches &c.*, Tome III, pp. 40–42.

28 See Charles Sellier: La tourelle de la Vieille-du-Temple, in *Bulletin de la Société de l'Histoire de Paris et de l'Ile-de-France*, 1887, pp. 148–164.

29 By Rudolf Wittkower in *Architectural Principles in the Age of Humanism*, London 1967.

30 Cf. Albert Lenoir: *Statistique Monumentale du Vieux Paris*, Paris 1867.

31 See below, chapter IV, part III, for Guillebert de Metz's description of the house of Jacques Duchié.

32 Quoted by Marcel Poëte: *Une Vie de Cité. Paris de sa naissance à nos jours*, II, Paris 1927, p. 124.

33 Dominque Hervier, op, cit., 1977, chapter IV, pp. 80–87.

34 See N. Sutherland: *The French Secretaries of State in the Age of Catherine de Medici*, London 1962.

35 There are a considerable number of contracts relating to this *hôtel* in this Minutier Central, étude LIV. For a summary of its history see Françoise Boudon, André Chastel, Hélène Couzy and Françoise Hamon: *Système de l'Architecture. Le Quartier des Halles à Paris*, Paris 1977, pp. 192–193.

36 See the forthcoming study on the Château de Madrid by Madame Monique Châtenet.

37 Cf. Louis Hautecoeur: *Histoire de l'Architecture classique en France*, Tome I, i, Paris 1963, pp. 447–452, and Simon Jervis: *Printed Furniture Designs before 1650*, London and Leeds 1974.

38 Cf. Louis Hautecoeur, op. cit., 1963, pp. 263–264.

39 Cf. Françoise Boudon *et al.*, op. cit., 1977, p. 217.

40 Cf. C. Lemaire: *Paris ancien et nouveau*, III, Paris 1685, pp. 290–291.

41 See Brantôme's portrait of her character.

42 Botticelli was not alone in choosing to show Venus riding on a shell. There are numerous Italian and Northern paintings and engravings of her in this pose of the sixteenth and seventeenth centuries. Cf. *Le Bartsch illustré*.

43 Cf. Mark Girouard: *Life in the English Country House. A Social and Architectural History*, New Haven and London, 1978, chapter 5.

Chapter III

1 Cf. Jean-Pierre Babelon: L'Urbanisme d'Henri IV et de Sully à Paris, in *L'Urbanisme de Paris et l'Europe 1600 1800* (Essays in honour of Pierre Francastel), Paris 1969.

2 See Jacques Thuillier: Economie et urbanisme au XVIIe siècle, in *Art de France*, pp. 311–312. Thuillier quotes a passage from Philippe de Béthune: *Le Conseiller d'Estat*, Paris 1633.

3 Cf. A. J. V. Le Roux de Lincy: Recherches historiques sur la chute et la reconstruction du pont Notre Dame à Paris (1499–1510), in *Bibliothèque de l'Ecole des Chartes*, 1845–1846, pp. 32–51. See also *Registres des délibérations du Bureau de la Ville, 1499–1628*, (Histoire générale de Paris), published by F. Bonnardot, S. Clemencet, P. Daudet, P. Guérin, L. Legrand, H. de Surirey de Saint Rémy, A. Tuetey, 19 vols, Paris 1883–1958.

4 Cf. Pierre Lavedan: *Histoire de l'Urbanisme à Paris*, Paris 1975, p. 150.

5 Marius Vachon: *La Renaissance française. L'Architecture nationale. Les Grands Maîtres Maçons*, Paris n.d., p. 59.

6 See *Registres des délibérations*, op. cit. above note 3, and the most complete documentary study remains A. J. V. Le Roux de Lincy: *Histoire de l'Hôtel de Ville*, Paris 1846.

7 Cf. Pierre Le Sueur: *Dominique de Cortone, dit le Boccador*, Paris 1928.

8 Cf. Marius Vachon: *Une Famille Parisienne des Maîtres Maçons aux XVe, XVIe et XVIIe siècles. Les Chambiges*, Paris 1907, pp. 111–128.

9 See *Registres des délibérations*, op. cit. above note 3.

10 This deliberately non-Italian architectural repertoire is much in evidence in Androuet du Cerceau's third *Livre d'Architecture* of 1582. See also de l'Orme's arguments for a French order of columns in his *Architecture,* Livre VI, chapitre XIII.

11 See Naomi Miller: The Form and Meaning of the Fontaine des Innocents, in *Art Bulletin,* 1968, pp. 270–277.

12 Cf. Sebastiano Serlio: *Libro Extraordinario,* Lyon 1551. A French-language edition was published simultaneously.

13 Cf. Paul Fréart de Chantelou: *Journal du Voyage du Cavalier Bernin en France,* edited by Ludovic Lalanne, Paris 1885 (reprinted Paris 1981), p. 48.

14 De Vigenère: *Suitte de Philostrate,* Paris 1602, f° 105 recto.

15 For example as at the Hôtel d'Etampes (Fig. 49) which seems to represent the end of a stylistic tradition begun at Blois.

16 See Ronsard's *Elegie à Pierre Lescot,* written about 1555, and published in 1560.

17 Etienne Jodelle's *Cléopatre captive* was first performed in 1552, and was admired by many at Court for its purity and for its fidelity to the form and tradition of Greek tragedy. See Pierre Champion: *Ronsard et son temps,* Paris 1925.

18 See Louis Batiffol: Les premières constructions de Pierre Lescot au Louvre d'après de nouveaux documents, in *Gazette des Beaux-Arts,* 1930, pp. 276–303, and in *Bulletin de la Société de l'Histoire de l'Art français,* 1930, pp. 86–90, and in *Procès verbaux de la Commission du Vieux Paris,* 1930, pp. 64–77. François Gebelin: Le Louvre de la Renaissance. Origine du Grand Dessein. La part de Jean Goujon, in *L'Architecture,* vol. XXXVI, 13, 1923. The theories in these articles were in part disproved by Christiane Aulanier: Le Palais du Louvre au XVIᵉ siècle. Documents inédits, in *Bulletin de la Société de l'Histoire de l'Art français,* 1951, pp. 85–100.

19 Cf. Pierre du Colombier: *Jean Goujon,* Paris 1949, chapter V.

20 Cf. Louis Hautecoeur: Le Louvre de Pierre Lescot, in *Gazette des Beaux Arts,* 15, 1927, pp. 199–218. Hautecoeur published a plan which he claimed to show Lescot's first, smaller project, but no later writer has been convinced by his view. See also Adolphe Berty: *Topographie historique du Vieux Paris. Région du Louvre et des Tuileries,* 2nd edition, Paris 1885, Vol. 1, chapter VI, pp. 201–217, 'Le Louvre sous François I de 1527 à 1547', for royal edicts concerning the Louvre.

21 Contract of 6 July 1582 (Archives Nationales, Minutier Central XC, 138). See chapter 3, part 2, of my forthcoming study on the Androuet du Cerceau.

22 See William McAllister Johnson and Victor E. Graham: Ronsard et 'La Renommée' du Louvre, in *Bibliothèque d'Humanisme et Renaissance,* 30, 1968, pp. 7–17.

23 Especially Alberti. A French translation of Alberti by Jean Martin was published in Paris in 1555. See Pierre Marœl: *Un vulgarisateur. Jean Martin,* Paris 1900.

24 See the drawing of the procession of Queen Louise de Lorraine leaving the Louvre through the central doorway, by Nicolas Houel of about 1578. Reproduced in Louis Hautecoeur: *Histoire du Louvre, 1200 1928,* Paris 1928, Fig. 26.

25 Lescot was unquestionably the architect of the screen of Saint-Germain-l'Auxerrois, the Louvre, the Fontaine des Innocents and the *hôtel* of the Maréchal Saint-André in the quartier des Halles. The attribution to Lescot of the château de Vallery for Saint-André is sound but not yet conclusive, as is the attribution to him of the gateway of the Hôtel des Ligneris/Carnavalet, see below, chapter 4, part 2.

26 Cf. La Croix du Maine: *Bibliothèque françoise,* Paris 1584.

27 The influence of Serlio at Vallery in the use of rustication is clear, but it is a rustication which is more finely designed than true Serlian 'rustic'. On Vallery see R. Planchenault: Les Châteaux de Vallery, in *Bulletin Monumental,* 1963.

28 The most complete, but by no means
    comprehensive, bibliography on the
    Louvre is in *Le Louvre et son quartier.
    800 ans d'histoire architecturale,*
    Catalogue of the exhibition at the
    Mairie Annexe du 1er Arrondissement
    (Délégation à l'Action artistique de la
    Ville de Paris), Paris 1982.

29 See Marianna Jenkins: 'The Imagery of
    the Henri II Wing of the Louvre', in
    *Journal of Medieval and Renaissance
    Studies,* 7, 1977, pp. 289–307.

30 Quoted in *Le Louvre et son quartier,*
    op. cit. above note 28, p. 22.

31 See Henri Lemonnier: 'Jean Goujon et
    la Salle des Cariatides au Louvre', in
    Gazette des Beaux-Arts, I, 1906,
    pp. 177–194, especially pp. 185–189.

32 The agreement of 1550 records 'Lesd.
    figures taillés de taille ronde selon et
    suivant ung modèle de plastre par cy
    devant faict et à luy livré par ledit sieur
    de Clagny (Pierre Lescot) . . .'

33 Anthony Blunt: *Art and Architecture in
    France, 1500–1700,* 1980 edition,
    chapter 3, note 17. 'This is perhaps the
    only design of Lescot which seems to
    go back directly to an Italian model, for
    both in their grouping and in their
    proportions the columns closely recall
    those in Giulio Romano's portico on
    the garden side of the Palazzo del Tè at
    Mantua.'

34 See the rapturous praise of the ceiling of
    the *chambre de parade* by Henri Sauval:
    Histoire et recherches &c., Tome II,
    pp. 35–36.

35 Cf. Maurice Roy: *Artistes et Monuments
    de la Renaissance en France,* I, Paris 1929,
    pp. 419–423, for the contract for the
    ceiling of 1556. See also Christiane
    Aulanier: La double origine du plafond
    de la Salle Henri II, in *Revue des Arts,*
    1954, n°2, pp. 109–114.

36 Cf. Henri Sauval, op. cit. above note
    34, p. 35.

37 I am grateful to Madame Catherine
    Grodecki for this information. For
    some of the problems posed by the
    texts of the contracts for the Louvre see
    Jean-Pierre Babelon: Bonnes et
    mauvaises lectures, in *Revue de l'Art,*
    n° 54, 1981, pp. 56–60, especially p. 59.

38 See Philibert de l'Orme, op. cit. Livre I,
    chapitres III–IV.

39 For Etienne Jodelle's artistic pretensions
    see *Oeuvres complètes,* edited by Enea
    Balmas, Vol. 1, Paris 1965, p. 176 and
    p. 184. He is to be associated with the
    design of the château de Verneuil for
    Philippe de Boulainvilliers. See poems
    dedicated to Boulainvilliers, Balmas
    ed., I, pp. 134–142, and chapter 3, part
    1, of my forthcoming study on the
    Androuet du Cerceau.

Chapter IV

1   For a bibliography of Italian, French,
    Flemish, Dutch and English editions of
    Serlio's books, see Julius Schlosser
    Magnino: *La letteratura artistica,*
    Florence 1977, pp. 418–420, the British
    Library and National Union
    Catalogues.

2   In his dedication of the *Livre des
    Grotesques* of 1566 to Renée de France,
    Androuet du Cerceau expressed the
    opinion that there was no longer a need
    to employ Italian artists in France.

3   Henri Estienne: *L'Introduction au Traitè
    de Conformité des merveilles anciennes aved
    les modernes, ou traité préparatif à
    l'Apologie pour Herodote,* Paris 1579, p.
    10: '. . . mon opinion est (sous
    correction) . . . prise de l'estime qu'on
    faisoit des ouvrages antiques,
    & principalement de ceux des peintres
    & sculpteurs. Car quand on parloit d'un
    tableau ou d'une statue d'ouvrage
    antique, on entendoit d'un ouvrage
    exquis: & par consequent qu'on tenoit
    fort cher, & qui estoit de grand pris.
    Et toutesfois ceci ne s'entendoit
    seulement des tableux d'Appeles, & de
    Zeuxis & des statues de Scopas, Myron,
    Praxiteles, & quelques autres de ce
    temps la (desquels les ouvrages estoyent
    encores en beaucoup plus grande estime
    que ne seroyent maintenant ceux de
    Dürer, Raphael, Michel l'Ange) mais
    aussi des ouvrages de plusieurs autres
    qui avoyent esté longtemps depuis.'

4   Cf. Jean Bodin: *Les Paradoxes
    Du Seigneur De Malestroict, Conseiller
    Du Roy, & Maistre ordinaire de ses
    competes, sur le faict des Monnoyes,
    presentez à sa Majesté, au mois de Mars,
    MDLXVI. Avec la réponse de M. Jean
    Bodin audicte paradoxes. Paris 1568.*

5   De Girard's titles as 'sécretaire des
    finances et historiographe du Roi' are
    given in Bibliothèque Nationale, ms.
    fr. 25730,

m° 589. See *Dictionnaire de Biographie française* Tome 12, Paris 1970, columns 4–5 for other details of his life.

6   Cf. *Le Secret des finances de France découvert et départi en trois livres par N. Fromenteau*, Paris 1581.

7   De La Noue, op. cit., pp. 164–166.

8   On Henri Sauval's life see the scholarly introduction by Michel Fleury to the 1974 reprint of the *Histoire et recherches des Antiquités de la Ville de Paris.*

9   Cf. Albert Buisson: *Le Chancelier Antione Duprat*, Paris 1935, p. 329.

10   See the engravings in A. Castellan: *Fontainebleau*, 1840, and Maurice Roy: 'Quelques Hôtels à Fontainebleau', in *Annales de la Société historique et archéologique du Gâtinais*, Tome XXVIII, 1910, pp. 51–74.

11   Both the Avery and Munich manuscripts contain drawings of the Hôtel de Ferrare and enlarged variants proposed by Serlio. See also François-Charles James: 'L'Hôtel de Ferrare à Fontainebleau d'après un document inédit', in *Actes du Colloque international sur l'art de Fontainebleau, 1972*, Paris 1975, pp. 35–37.

12   Cf. Philibert de l'Orme: *Architecture,* Livre VIII, chapitre XV.

13   Recorded by Androuet du Cerceau in a drawing in the British Museum.

14   'Quanto al designo poi che la mi demanda da la mia casa di Fontanableo . . . credo che sia più tosto per esser fatta nel luogo, dove è, et dove par che sia più di quel che vi convegneria, et per esservisi osservato anco un poco più le misure et ordini del architettura, cosi nel francese come in quel che ci è del Italiano, che nin si sogliono cosi avvertire et osservare in quelle di questi paesi, che perchè in effetto sia cosa segnalata nè notabile. Et mr Bastian Serlio, che ne è stato l'architetto l'havea messa in un suo libro d'architettura, che ha ultimamente fatto et che vuol far stampare, Et io ne l'ho fatto levare, parendomi che'l vederla in disegno fusse per levarle più tosto, che per darle punto di riputatione, Ma se V. Ex. la vorrà pur qualella è, non manchero d'ubidirla cosi in questo, come in quel tutto, che la mi comanderà sempre et gliela mandero, il che anco non saprei far per adesso per non esser in luogo commodo . . .' Letter to the Duke of Ferrara from Cardinal Ippolito d'Este of 16 October 1546.

15   See Jean-Pierre Babelon, art. cit., *Revue de l'Art*, 1978, p. 97.

16   Cf. David Coffin: *The Villa d'Este at Tivoli*, Princeton 1960.

17   Cf. Peter Thornton: *Seventeenth Century Interior Decoration in England, France and Holland*, New Haven and London 1978, chapter III, and Mark Girouard: *Life in the English Country House. A Social and Architectural History*, New Haven and London 1978, chapter 5.

18   See below, chapter 4, part III.

19   Cf. Wolfram Prinz: *Die Entstehung der Galerie in Frankreich und Italien*, Berlin 1970, and reviews of Herr Prinz's book by Volker Hoffmann in *Architectura*, 1971, pp. 102 112 and by Frank Büttner in *Architectura*, 1972, pp. 75–80.

20   Cf. Saugrain: *Curiositez de Paris*, Paris 1716, p. 4.

21   See below, chapter 4, part 3.

22   Jean-Pierre Babelon, art. cit., *Revue de l'Art*, 1978, p. 91.

23   Especially the Porte Saint Antoine, designed by Métezeau and built in 1585, which stood close to the Bastille.

24   Jean-Pierre Babelon, art. cit., *Revue de l'Art*, 1978, pp. 86–87. Des Ligneris ordered building work to be begun in 1546, but only signed the contract in 1548. The excavation and building of the substantial cellars (Fig. 84) might well have taken up a great deal of the time between 1546 and the contract of 3 June 1548.

25   See Allan Braham and Peter Smith: *François Mansart*, London 1972, pp. 250–52.

26   Henri Sauval, op. cit., Tome III, p. 12.

27   See Lionello Puppi: *Michele Sanmicheli, architetto di Verona*, Padua 1971.

28   Especially drawings datable to the 1570s, such as in the album in the Pierpont Morgan Library, New York. See chapter IV, part 2, of my study on Androuet du Cerceau.

29 Cf. Hubert Jedin: *Geschichte des Konzils von Trient*, Band II, Freiburg 1957, p. 153. Des Ligneris was one of three orators in his capacity as a jurist. With him were Claude d'Urfé and Pierre Danès.

30 See Michel Gallet and Bernard de Montgolfier: L'Hôtel de Carnavalet, Ses Hôtes, Ses Bâtiments, Sa Décoration sculptée, in *Bulletin du Musée Carnavalet*, 1974, nᵒs 1–2.

31 Archives Nationales, Minutier Central XIX, 170 and 175, contracts of 6 March 1547 and 16 May 1548.

32 'Item faire ung corps de logis en lad. place de vingt deux piedz dedans euvre et suyvant led. dessin de ce fait que sera de pareilles espoisseurs que celluy de Benoist Legrant, sr du Plessis, assis en la rue des Poullies, ou de plus grosses espesseurs si les ouvraiges le requierent, et aussi de pareilles facons et matieres que celluy de monsieur Challopin, assis près le jeu de paulme de Bracque. Et y aura aud. corps de logis cinq assises de pierre dure au rez de chaussée aux deux pans, dont la cinqième portera retraicte, et les croisées, pilastres et autres moullures dud. corps de logis seront de pierre de St. Leu de la mesme sorte et facon que celles qui sont aud. corps de logis dud. Challopin.'

33 Archives Nationales, Minutier Central, XIX, 94. 'Et avecques ce luy faire chassys de bois a mectre pappier pour led croisées et demys croisées, portans, coullisseaulx, ou sera ordonné par led. Berthelemy . . .'

34 Archives Nationales, Minutier Central, XIX, 91, contract of 10 July 1546.

35 The contract specifies the kitchen dimensions as '23 pieds de long sur 14 de large, aved garde manger, chambre au dessus, reliée au corps d'hôtel par une galerie ouverte, surmontée d'une autre galerie pour desservir le corps de logis.'

36 Archives Nationales, Minutier Central XIX, 184. Contract of 13 April 1551.

37 On Antoine Sanguin's buildings and fortune see Jules Lair: La seigneurie de Bares, in *Mémoires de la Société de Paris et de l'Ile-de-France,* Tome II, 1876, pp. 208–211, and on the ancient roots of the Sanguin family in Paris see Lebeuf: *Histoire du Diocèse de Paris,* Tome VIII, p. 374. On the *hôtel's* dates and owners see Robert Laulan: Note rectificative sur l'Hôtel de la Force, in *Bulletin de la Société de l'Histoire de Paris et de l'Ile-de-France,* 1960–1961, pp. 62–65.

38 See Pierre de l'Estoile: *Journal* for 26 January 1580. Birague's gallery on the north side of the garden still exists.

39 See Jean-Pierre Babelon: De l'Hôtel d'Albret à l'Hôtel d'O, in *Bulletin de la Société de l'Histoire de Paris et de l'Ile-de-France,* 1970, p. 93.

40 For example the Hôtel de Nemours, parts of which have survived the cutting of the rue de Nemours.

41 The Hôtel de Bouchage, see below.

42 Cf. Bella Bessard and Sylvie Béguin: L'Hôtel du Faur dit Torpanne, in *Revue de l'Art*, 1968, pp. 38–56.

43 Cf. Sylvie Béguin: La Galerie du Connetable de Montmorency à l'Hôtel de la rue Sainte-Avoye, in *Bulletin de la Société de l'Histoire de l'Art français,* 1977, pp. 47–65, and on dell'Abbate's range of activity see Sylvie Béguin: Niccolo dell'Abbate en France, in *Art de France,* II, 1962, pp. 113 146.

44 Jean-Pierre Babelon, art. cit., *Revue de l'Art*, 1978, p. 108, note 95.

45 See the study of the partnership of the humanist Gabriel Symioni and Antoine Duprat, for the sculptural embellishment of Duprat's house at Vanves just outside Paris, by Lilliane Châtelet Lange: 'Le Museo di Vanves' (1560). Collections de sculptures et musées au XVIᵉ siècle en France', in *Zeitschrift für Kunstgeschichte,* 1975, pp. 266–285. The largest cycle of sculpture for a country house was for Verneuil, for which a contract has been discovered of 1560 between the owner Philippe de Boulainvilliers and the sculptor Ponce Jacquio. The contract is for forty statues, and the idea might have come from Boulainvilliers' friend, the poet Etienne Jodelle. See the ten engravings of Verneuil in *Le Premier Volume des plus excellents Bastiments de France* of 1576 by Androuet du Cerceau, and chapter 3, part 1, of my study on du Cerceau.

46 Cf. Maurice Roy: *Artistes et Monuments de la Renaissance en France,* Vol. 1, Paris 1929, chapter 9 on Anet, pp. 285–319.

47 Cf. Maurice Roy, op. cit., 'Les travaux de Philibert de l'Orme à Paris, 1546–1559,' pp. 348–366.

48 Cf. Jean-Pierre Babelon: 'Sur trois hôtels du Marais, à Paris, datant du règne de Henri III,' in *Bulletin Monumental*, 1977, pp. 223–230.

49 Cf. Michel Le Moël: 'L'Hôtel de Marle au Marais,' in *Gazette des Beaux Arts*, 25, 1970, pp. 213–224.

50 See chapter XVIII of de l'Orme's *Nouvelles Inventions pour Bien Bastir à petits fraiz.*

51 On de Vigenère see Denis Métral: *Blaise de Vigenère, archéologue et critique d'art*, Paris 1939. Nevers founded a magnificent library which required two librarians, Métral, op. cit. p. 217. See the *témoinages* in tribute to Nevers in Guy Coquille's *Poemata*, Nevers 1590.

52 On the later history of the Hôtel de Nevers see Allan Braham and Peter Smith: *François Mansart*, London 1972, p. 238.

53 Cf. Jean-Pierre Babelon: La maison de Jacques Coeur à Paris, 38–42 rue des Archives. Sa place dans l'architecture brique et pierre, in *Procès-verbaux de la Commission du Vieux Paris*, 4 October 1971, pp. 10–26.

54 Cf. David Thomson: A note on Pierre Lescot the painter, in *Burlington Magazine*, 1978, pp. 666–667, p. 667, note 6.

55 Cf. Josianne Sartre: *Châteaux 'brique et pierre' en France*, Paris 1981, p. 55.

56 See my forthcoming study on the Androuet du Cerceau, chapter 3, part 2.

57 See the painting by Abraham de Verwer of 1637 in the Musée Carnavalet, and Poinsart's engraving of the Hôtel de Nevers, reproduced by Braham and Smith, op. cit.

58 Cf. Jean-Pierre Babelon: 'Les hôtels de Sandreville, d'Alméras et Poussepin. Etude topographique et architecturale sur le lotissement du parc du Cardinal Bertrand, 24 à 36 rue des Francs-Bourgeois, 1 à 7 rue Elzévier, 1 à 9 rue Barbette (3ᵉ)', in *Bulletin de la Société de l'Histoire de Paris et de l'Ile-de-France*, 1972–1973, pp. 63–107, especially pp. 67–78.

59 Cf. Jean-Pierre Babelon: 'Notices historiques sur les immeubles traités par la SO. RE. MA. dans l'ilot Payene Elzévir: n° 2, 4 et 6 rue Elzévir, 22 et 20 rue des Francs-Bourgeois, et 1, 3, 5 et 7 rue Payenne', in *Procès Verbaux de la Commission du Vieux Paris*, 1 March 1971, p. 33–51, especially pp. 39–42.

60 Cf. Edouard Jacques Ciprut: 'L'Architecte du Palais Abbatial de Saint Germain des Prés,' in *Bulletin de la Société de l'Histoire de l'Art français*, 1956, pp. 218–21.

61 Cf. Jean-Pierre Babelon: 'L'Urbanisme d'Henri IV et Sully à Paris,' in *L'Urbanisme de Paris et l'Europe 1600 1800* (Essays in honour of Pierre Francastel), Paris 1969.

62 Cf. Maurice Dumolin: L'Hôtel de Condé, in *Bulletin de la Société historique du VIᵉ arrondissement*, 1925, pp. 18–57, especially pp. 24–28.

63 Documentary histories of the site are given by Charles Sellier: *Anciens Hôtels de Paris*, Paris 1910, pp. 355–396 and by Maurice Dumolin: *Etudes de topographie parisienne*, Tome III, Paris 1931, pp. 376–387. See also Robert Dauvergne: 'Une Grande Demeure au Marais en 1650. L'Hôtel du Duc d'Angoulême,' in *Bulletin de la Société de l'Histoire de Paris et de l'Ile-de-France*, *1957–1959*, pp. 83–89.

64 Sellier, op. cit., p. 370.

65 Cf. Catherine Grodecki: 'La Construction du Château de Wideville et sa place dans l'architecture française du dernier quart du XVIᵉ siècle,' in *Bulletin Monumental*, 1978, pp. 135–175.

66 I am grateful to Monsieur François Charles James for this information. On the Métezeau family of architects see Pierre du Colombier, 'Autour des Métezeau' in *Bibliothèque d'Humanisme et Renaissance*, 1943, pp. 182–183.

67 Sellier, op. cit., p. 360.

68 Henri Sauval: *Histoire et recherches des Antiquités de la Ville de Paris*, Tome II, Paris 1724, p. 241. See Jean-Pierre Babelon: 'De l'Hôtel d'Albret à l'Hôtel d'O. Etude topographique d'une partie de la Culture Sainte-Catherine, 29 bis à 47 rue des Francs Bourgeois; 48 à 50 rue Vieille-du-Temple, 14 et 16 rue des Rosiers,' in *Bulletin de la Société de*

l'Histoire de Paris et de l'Ile-de-France, 1970, pp. 87–145, especially pp. 138–141. A photograph of a corner of the courtyard in a dilapidated and much altered condition can be seen in Georges Pillement: *Demeures parisiennes en péril,* Paris 1948, p. 11.

69 Archives Nationales, Minutier Central, XC, 146.

70 *See Catalogue of the Drawings of the R.I.B.A., Jacques Gentilhâtre, compiled by Rosalys Coope,* London 1972.

71 The activity of Baptiste Androuet du Cerceau as an architect of town houses is described in chapter 3, part 2, of my study on the Androuet du Cerceau.

72 See above, chapter 1, note 1.

73 On the Hôtel de Montmorency see Léon Mirot, 'L'Hôtel et les collections du Connétable de Montmorency' in *Bibliothèque de l'Ecole des Chartes,* 1918, especially pp. 347–369. On the Hôtel de Guise, see for plans and references Jean-Pierre Babelon: Nouveaux documents pour la restauration de l'Hôtel de Guise, 58 rue des Archives, in *La Vie Urbaine,* July–September 1965, (fascicule 3). On the Hôtel of Claude Gouffier, seigneur de Boissy, the builder of the magnificent château de Oiron in Poitou, see François-Charles James 'L'Hôtel de Mayenne avant son acquisition par Charles de Lorraine,' in *Bulletin de la Société de l'Histoire de Paris et de l'Ile de France,* 1970, pp. 43–85, especially the plan on p. 82.

74 Cf. Armand de Bourbon, Prince de Conti, *'Mémoires de Monseigneur le prince de Conty touchant la conduite de sa maison. Publié par le Sieur de Vigan,'* Paris 1669 (in 12°, 108 pp.), London edition 1711.

75 A modernized version of the text was published by Pierre Champion, *La vie de Paris au Moyen Age. Splendeurs et misères de Paris (XIVe–XVe siècles),'* Paris 1934, pp. 18–19. For the original see A. J. V. Le Roux de Lincy and L. M. Tisserand, *'Paris et ses historiens aux XIVe et XVe siècles,'* Paris 1866, pp. 199–200.

76 See A. J. V. Le Roux de Lincy, op. cit.

77 See Audiger: *La Maison reglée et l'art de diriger la maison d'un grand seigneur tant à la ville qu'à la campagne,* Paris 1692 and Claude Fleury, *Les Devoirs des maîtres et des domestiques,* Amsterdam 1688.

Of interest is W. H. Wiley, *The Gentleman of Renaissance France,* Cambridge (Mass.) 1954.

78 Cf. Hugh Murray Baillie, 'Etiquette and the planning of the State Apartments in Baroque Palaces,' in *Archaeologia,* Vol. CI, 1967, pp. 167–199.

79 See M. N. Tommaseo: *Relations des Ambassadeurs Vénitiens,* Tome II, Paris 1838, p. 567.

80 Cf. Louis Claude Douët-d'Arcq, *Comptes de l'hôtel des Rois de France aux XIVe et XVe siècles,* Paris 1865, p. VII and p. IX.

81 Cf. *Historical Manuscripts Commission, Salisbury (Cecil) Mss.* London 1889, iii, p. 75.

82 Cf. Pierre Couperie, 'Les marchés de pourvoierie: viandes et poissons chez les grands au XVIIe siècle,' in *Pour une histoire de l'alimentation. Receuil des travaux présentés par Jean Jacques Hémardinquer. Cahier des Annales, 28.* Paris 1970, pp. 241–253, and *Pratiques et discours alimentaires de la Renaissance. Actes du colloque de Tours 1979,* edited by J. C. Margolin and R. Sauzet.

83 Cf. Description de Paris par Thomas Platter le Jeune de Bale (1599), in *Mémoires de la Société de l'Histoire de Paris et de l'Ile de France,* Tome XXIII, 1896, pp. 167–224, especially p. 172 and p. 203.

84 Cf. Alfred Franklin: *Paris et les Parisiens au XVI siècle. Paris physique. Paris social. Paris intime.* Paris 1921, pp. 394–395.

85 Cf. Laurent Joubert: 'De la Santé du Prince,' in *Erreurs populaires touchant la médicine,* Paris 1579, p. 622.

86 Cf. Pierre Le Muet: *Augmentations de nouveaux Bastiments faits en France par les Ordres et Desseins du Sieur le Muet,* Paris 1647, pl. 2.

87 Cf. Jean-Pierre Babelon, art. cit., *Revue de l'Art,* 1978, pp. 87–89.

88 Brantôme, IX, p. 296.

89 The King's stables were north west of the Louvre on the south side of the rue Saint-Honoré, and Diane de France's stables were on the corner of the rue de la Lamproie (now rue des Rosiers) on the site marked D in Fig. 18.

90 The second owner of the Hôtel du Cardinal de Meudon, was the Chancellor René de Birague. A supplement to his will of 2 November 1583 (Archives Nationales, Minutier Central, CIX, 70, pièces 133–134) is a list of sums of money left to the 46 people in his service, of whom 3 were equerries, 5 were grooms and 3 were responsible for mules. For Birague and his magnificent tomb by Germain Pilon see Catherine Grodecki: Les marchés de Germain Pilon pour la chapelle funéraire et les tombeaux des Birague en l'église Sainte-Catherine du Val des écoliers, in Revue de l'Art, 54, 1981,
pp. 61–78. Cecil's portrait is reproduced in David Cecil: The Cecils of Hatfield House, London, 1973.

91 J. A. De Thou: Mémoires . . . depuis 1553 jusqu'en 1601, Petitot edition (Collection des mémoires complètes, &c., 1er série, tome XXXVII), p. 399.

92 Cf. M. Deloche: La Maison de Richelieu, Paris 1912, p. 321.

93 See Peter Thornton: Seventeenth-Century Interior Decoration in England, France and Holland, New Haven and London 1978.

94 See Henry Havard: Dictionnaire de l'ameublement, 4 vols, Paris 1887–1890, entry on 'natte'.

95 Jean-Pierre Babelon, art. cit., Revue de l'Art, 1978, p. 87.

Chapter V

1 For example Verneuil and Charleval.

2 For the 1582 contracts for the building of the western half of the cour carrée, which name Baptiste Androuet du Cerceau as the architect instructed to follow Pierre Lescot's plans for the ensemble, see chapter III, part 2, of my forthcoming book on the du Cerceau.

3 See Tony Sauvel's lecture of 19 October 1966, in Bulletin de la Société Nationale des Antiquaires de France.

4 The fullest study of the building of the Pont-Neuf is François Boucher: Le Pont-Neuf, 2 vols, Paris 1925–1926.

5 On the Tuileries see Anthony Blunt: Philibert de l'Orme, London 1958. Tony Sauvel, 'Recherches sur les ressources dont Catherine de Médicis a disposé pour construire les Tuileries,' in Bulletin de la Société de l'Histoire de l'Art française, 1967. Denis André Chevallay: Der grosse Tuilerienentwurf in der Überlieferung Du Cerceaus (Kieler Kunsthistorische Studien, Band 3), 1973, and Liliane Châtelet-Lange: 'La "forma ovale si come costumarono li antichi romani": salles et cours ovales en France au seizième siècle,' in Architecture, 1976, pp. 128–147, especially pp. 139–144.

6 See my forthcoming study on the du Cerceau, chapter IV, part 2, and also the larger projects published in the Livre d'Architecture of 1559 and 1582.

7 For a census of recent literature see Anne-Marie Lecoq, 'La città festeggiante. Les fêtes publiques aux XVe et XVIe siècles,' in Revue de l'Art, 33, 1976, pp. 83–100. Studies on the most important late Valois festivals held in Paris are The Entry of Henri II into Paris, 16 June 1549, Facsimile with an introduction by I. D. McFarlane, (Medieval and Renaissance texts and studies, vol. 7), Binghamton, New York 1982. Victor E. Graham and William McAllister Johnson, The Paris Entries of Charles IX and Elisabeth of Austria, 1571, Toronto 1974. Le Balet Comique by Balthazar de Beaujoyeulx, 1581, Facsimile and an introduction by Margaret M. McGowan (Medieval and Renaissance texts and studies, vol. 6), Binghamton, New York 1982.

8 D. A. Chevallay, op. cit. above note 5. For the argument against the oval halls having been intended to house baths and a grotto see Liliane Châtelet-Lange, art. cit. above note 5, p. 142, note 55.

9 See my forthcoming study on the du Cerceau, chapter III, part 2.

10 On de l'Orme's 'sixth order' and for designs by seventeenth- and eighteenth-century architects for a 'French order' see J.-M. Pérouse de Monclos, 'Le Sixième Ordre d'Architecture, ou la Pratique des Ordres suivant les Nations,' in Journal of the Society of Architectural Historians, vol. XXXVI, 1977, pp. 223–240.

11 See my forthcoming study on the du Cerceau, chapter III, part 2.

12 See Adolphe Berty: *Topographie du Vieux Paris. Région du Louvre et des Tuileries*, I, Paris 1885, p. 258–264.

13 See also Tony Sauvel, art. cit. above note 3.

14 A second edition was published in 1568.

15 An outline of de l'Orme and Bullant's years in Rome is given by Volker Hoffmann: Artisti francesi a Roma: Philibert de l'Orme e Jean Bullant, in *Colloqui del Sodalizio,* (Seconda serie), 4, 1973–1974, pp. 55–68.

16 See the full account by Jean-Pierre Babelon, 'Les Travaux de Henri IV au Louvre et aux Tuileries,' in *Paris et Ile-de-France. Mémoires publiés par la Féderation des Sociétés historiques et archéologiques de Paris et de l'Ile-de-France,* Tome 25, 1978, pp. 55–130.

17 See François-Charles James, 'Jean Bullant. Recherches sur l'architecture française du XVIᵉ siècle,' in *Ecole Nationale des Chartes. Positions des thèses.* 1968, pp. 101–109, and Françoise Boudon, André Chastel, Hélène Couzy and Françoise Hamon, *'Système de l'Architecture urbaine. Le Quartier des Halles à Paris,'* Paris 1977, chapter IV on aristocratic architecture and the development of the parish of Saint Eustache.

18 See F–C. James, art. cit. above note 17, p. 108.

19 For the plan attached to the 1582 contract see Boudon, Chastel, Couzy and Hamon, op. cit. above, note 17, p. 232, fig. 308.

20 See E. Bonnaffé, *Inventaire des meubles de Catherine de Médicis en 1589*, Paris 1874.

21 See Frances Yates: *The Valois Tapestries*, London 1959, p. 122.

22 'un cabinet apelé des miroirs' containing 'cent dix neuf miroirs plains de Venize enchasséz dans le lambris dudict cabinet'. For the history of the use of mirror glass in decoration in France see Henry Havard: *Dictionnaire de l'Ameublement et la Décoration,* Paris, n.d., vol. II, cols 1100–1116.

23 For archive references to the building contracts relating to the Hôtel de la Reine see Boudon, Chastel, Couzy and Hamon, op. cit., p. 195, and for the seventeenth-century building campaigns see Rosalys Coope: *Salomon de Brosse,* London 1972, pp. 251–252.

24 See Françoise Boudon: 'Urbanisme et speculation à Paris au XVIIIᵉ siècle, Le Terrain de l'Hôtel de Soissons', in *Journal of the Society of Architectural Historians,* 1973, pp. 267–307.

25 See Jean-Pierre Babelon: 'Nouveaux Documents sur la Place Dauphine et ses abords', in *Commission du Vieux Paris. Procès-verbaux,* 1966, pp. 32–44, especially p. 33. This article gives a full bibliography.

Conclusion

1 Savot, op. cit., p. 18.

2 The term 'gothic' was used by Blondel as a general term of disapproval. See for example his annotations to Louis Savot's bibliography, Savot, op. cit., pp. 338–357, where the reader will be surprised to see Serlio's work on the orders described as 'gothic'.

3 J.-F. Blondel: *Architecture Françoise*, IV, pp. 64–66. On J.-F. Blondel see E. Kaufmann, 'The Contribution of J.-F. Blondel to Mariette's *Architecture française*', in *Art Bulletin,* XXXI, 1949, 58, and J. Lejeaux, 'Jacques-François Blondel, professeur d'architecture', in *L'Architecture,* XL, 1947, 23.

4 See Louis Hautecoeur, *Le Louvre et les Tuileries de Louis XIV,* Paris 1927, pp. 123–126.

5 J.-F. Blondel, op. cit., IV, p. 83, '. . . il falloit nécessairement détruire l'ouvrage de Philibert de l'Orme, ou chercher à concilier le neuf avec l'ancien, pour composer un Edifice plus conforme aux loix de bon goût, & plus digne de la splendeur du regne de Louis le Grand . . .'

6 On Parisian churches see Amédée Boinet: *Les Eglises Parisiennes,* 3 vols, Paris 1958–1964.

7 Sauval, op. cit., I, p. 437. 'This great elevation of columns and plethora of mouldings, which are not to be seen anywhere else, this stupendous length of pilasters and heightening of the

vaults which are the most defective features of its architecture. . . . Truly there are some column capitals in the portal of the aisle, whose leaf decoration are most delicate and which are the most beautiful in Paris and the best, if they were not a little gothic towards the top. There are some in a similar style and as good on the left side, and that is the only good thing to be found in this church.'

8   For the quotation and the best published photographs of the interior of Saint Eustache see Michel Fleury, Alain Erlande-Brandenburg and Jean-Pierre Babelon: *Paris Monumental,* Paris 1974, pp. 152–153.

9   Sauval, op. cit., p. 461.

10 See Père Louis Beurrier: *Histoire du monastère et couvent des Pères Célestins de Paris* &c., Paris 1634, and Françoise Isaac, 'Les Célestins de Paris. Etude historique et archéologique,' in *Ecole Nationale des Chartes. Positions des Thèses,* 1965, pp. 43–50.

11 Archives Nationales, Minutier Central, XIX, 158.

12 ibid.

13 See Maurice Roy, *Artistes et Monuments de la Renaissance en France,* I, 1929, pp. 1–120.

14 See Maurice Roy, op. cit., I, p. 143.

15 See Françoise Boudon, Françoise Hamon and Sylvia Pressouyre 'La Chapelle Saint-Eloi des Orfèvres,' in *Bibliothèque d'Humanisme et Renaissance,* XXVIII, 1966, pp. 427–438.

16 Boudon *et al.,* art. cit., Fig. 12.

17 See Rudolf Wittkower: *Architectural Principles in the Age of Humanism,* London 1967.

18 'con piu maturo consiglio jo lodo si faccia questa colonna piana di ordine dorico: e sopra esta sia una fascia che rinciga tutta l'opera.'

19 On the Cordeliers see Laure Beaumont-Maillet, *Le Couvent des Cordeliers de Paris. Etude historique et archéologique, du XIIIᵉ siècle à nos jours,* Paris 1975.

20 Philibert de l'Orme in the *Architecture* says no more of this design than 'Nous figurons cy-après une autre sorte de porte, que nous appellerons Corinthienne, ou de l'ordre composé, & luy donnerons deux fois sa largeur pour sa hauteur, & quelque chose davantage. Qui la voudroit faire belle & de bonne grace, ainsi que j'ay dict & en ay veu plusieurs, il luy faudroit donner par les costez autant de largeur qu'est toute l'ouverture de sa limière. Comme quoy? vous prendrez toute la largeur où vois voulez faire vostre portail, ou grande porte, & la diviserez en trois parties, desquelles vous en donnerez une à la largeur de la lumiere de la porte, & les deux autres à une chacune partie par les costez. Si vous voulez faire une chose bien convenable & belle, faites que tout l'ornement de la porte ne soit plus haut depuis le dessus de la corniche jusques à l'aire, que toute la largeur de la porte avec ses ornements. Il faut que cela soit d'un quarré parfaict. Par les costez vous pourrez ériger des colomnes, piliers striez & cannelez, ou autrement: & entre iceaux faire des niches, telles que je veux monstrer par l'exemple d'une grande porte accompagnée de ses ornements: laquelle je fis faire par commandement (il y a huict ans passez) pour servir à quelque sale de triomphe: mais, helas, ce triomphe peu après fut converty en grandissime desolation & desastre, duquel nous nous ressentons encores. Quant à l'explication & sens moral des histoires de ladite porte, nous n'en parlerons en ce lieu, esperant les produire ailleurs, & beaucoup plus à propos. Je reprendray donc notre porte Corinthienne, & diray franchement qu'elle se peut faire beaucoup plus riche que les Doriques, ou Ioniques: car elle est propre & bien à propos pour y mettre plusieurs ornements & devises, tant aux frizes, qu'acroteres & amortissements, ainsi que vous le pouvez juger par la figure qui vous en est proposée cy-après.'

21 See for example John Constable's lecture on 'mannerists' in R. B. Beckett: *John Constable's Discourses* (Suffolk Records Society), Vol. XIV, Ipswich 1970, pp. 57–58.

22 Du Bellay, op. cit., livre I, chapitre XI.

Bibliographical Note

The historical, social, topographical and administrative literature of Paris is enormous. Many of the references given in the notes of this study could have been doubled or tripled in length, but the temptation has been resisted. The reader seeking to verify facts or question hypotheses in the text should find references in the notes to be to books and articles which are thorough within their own stated aims and limitations.

No better introduction to France in the sixteenth century could be recommended than J. H. M. Salmon's *Society in Crisis. France in the Sixteenth Century*, London 1975, which has a useful bibliography of printed sources and modern studies. Bernard Rouleau's *Le Tracé des Rues de Paris. Formation, typologie, fonctions*, Paris 1975, is an excellent survey of the development of Paris from antiquity to modern times, with numerous plans and diagrams, and a thorough account of cartographical sources. Jacques Hillairet *Dictionnaire des rues de Paris*, 2 vols + supplement, Paris 1979, should be used with caution, for there are frequent important omissions and mistakes, and contains no references.

Architecture has been a preoccupation of only a few of the many nineteenth- and twentieth-century topographical historians of Paris. The basis of much modern architectural and topographical research remains Adolphe Berty and others: *Histoire générale de Paris. Topographie historique du Vieux Paris* (revised, annotated and completed by L. M. Tisserand and others), 6 vols, 2nd edition, Paris 1885–1897. 1–2, *Région du Louvre et des Tuileries*, 3, *Région du bourg Saint Germain*, 4, *Région du faubourg Saint Germain*, 5, *Région occidentale de l'Université*, 6, *Région centrale de l'Université*. Many areas not covered by Berty (such as the Marais) were the subject of Maurice Dumolin's *Etudes de topographie parisienne*, 3 vols, Paris 1929–1931.

The outstanding modern authority on the history of Paris and her architecture is Monsieur Jean-Pierre Babelon whose *Demeures parisiennes sous Henri IV et Louis XIII*, Paris 1965, and numerous articles referred to in the Notes, have transformed our knowledge and appreciation of every phase of post-medieval domestic building in Paris. The suite to M. Babelon's book is Michel Gallet's excellent *Paris Domestic Architecture of the Eighteenth Century*, London 1972.

The study of the architectural, demographic and social history of Paris has been greatly enriched by Françoise Boudon, André Chastel, Hélène Couzy and Françoise Hamon's book *Système de l'Architecture urbaine. Le Quartier des Halles à Paris*, Paris 1977. This remarkable and original book not only documents in detail the physiognomy of the *quartier des Halles*, but provides a model of methodology which should influence specialists in various aspects of urban history of all nationalities.

No volumes have appeared to date in the series *Nouvelle Histoire de Paris* dealing with the sixteenth or seventeenth century, but all of those which have been published contain good texts and useful bibliographies. Jean Favier's contribution *Paris au XVe siècle, 1380–1500*, Paris 1974, especially chapter III, 'Demeures parisiennes', is a helpful architectural and demographic preface to the period covered here. Pierre Lavedan's *Histoire de l'Urbanisme à Paris*, is a part of the series, and tells the story of Parisian urban planning from antiquity to modern times.

This study might be accused of treating the architecture, and some aspects of the social history of Paris in a vacuum. The reader will have the right to feel dismayed at the absence of references to books and to articles dealing with French provincial cities, or cities outside France especially in Italy. The publications of the Inventaire Générale des Monuments et des richesses artistiques de la France will eventually provide a comprehensive documentation of the architecture of the regions, towns and cities of France, but at the time of writing the only French city to have received a thorough modern study is Aix-en-Provence with Jean Jacques Gloton's *Renaissance et Baroque à Aix-en-Provence*, 2 vols, Rome 1979. Of great interest is the series *Le città nella storia d'Italia* (Editori Laterza) in which studies on Genoa by

209

Ennio Poleggi and Paola Cevini, on Rome by Italo Insolera, Bologna by G. Ricci and Florence by G. Fanelli have appeared, with many more volumes promised. Despite long reflection, few exact points of comparison can be made between an Italian city and the architectural history of Paris during the sixteenth century.

This book would have been greatly improved if an equivalent to J. Delumeau's *Vie économique et sociale de Rome dans la seconde moitié du XVIe siècle,* Paris 1957–1959 had been written on Paris. Roland Mousnier in his *La stratification sociale à Paris aux XVIIe et XVIIIe siècles,* Paris 1976, provides much demographic information on the next century which complements some of the observations made in these pages.

Without the Bibliothèque historique de la Ville de Paris, housed in Diane de France's *hôtel,* work on any aspect of the history of Paris would be more cumbersome. With complete sets of all the journals of Parisian historical societies on open access, and comprehensive subject and topographical card indexes of books and articles, the research for this book has been made much easier.

After the text of this book was sent to the printers Barbara B. Diefendorf's *Paris City Councillors in the Sixteenth Century. The Politics of Patrimony,* Princeton 1983, was published. Her chapter 'Urban residences and rural properties', pp. 59–71, contains several observations and pieces of information which I would have liked to incorporate in the part of this book on households. On page 64 we read 'Though it was not until the seventeenth century that it became the fashion among the wealthy nobles of the robe to have elegant town houses, built of stone like miniature castles around a cour d'honneur, at least some of the sixteenth century Parisian élite must already have had large and luxurious houses.' I hope that the architectural history of sixteenth-century Paris, as told in these pages, will enhance the work and be of interest to social and economic historians.

Index